why are
conservatives
always wrong?

Guy — In case
you have

trouble.

starting   ⊙
conversations.

—Douglas

why are
conservatives
always
wrong?

TERRIFYING
QUOTES FROM
CONSERVATIVES
THROUGHOUT
U.S. HISTORY

douglas ting

EDITOR

TILIKUM PRESS · PORTLAND

TILIKUM PRESS
wacaw.book@gmail.com

Printed in the United States of America

First Printing, 2015

ISBN 978-0-9968214-2-1

Library of Congress Control Number: 2015916273

Photography credits are found on page 295.
Book design by K. M. Weber, www.ilibribookdesign.com

FOR **BENJAMIN TING**

what have conservatives said about ...

Introduction ix

Slavery 1

Native Americans 20

Imperialism and the American Empire 34

Women's Suffrage 44

Jim Crow and Segregation 60

Immigration 90

Civil Rights 110

Freedom to Marry 136

Sexual Privacy 160

Women's Bodies and Rights 172

A Special Section on Richard Nixon 186

Religion and Government 192

War 200

Economic Regulation 220

Science and the Environment 248

Natural Disasters 280

Epilogue 291

Introduction

In 2015, the U.S. Supreme Court legalized marriage equality in America. The Court, in *Obergefell v. Hodges*, invali-
dated the anti-gay marriage statutes of thirteen states
and recognized what a majority of Americans already felt,
that the freedom to marry should not be denied based on
sexual orientation. Almost fifty years before, the Supreme
Court in *Loving v. Virginia* (1967) granted the fundamental
right of marriage to interracial couples. Before that, anti-
miscegenation laws in sixteen states prevented interracial
marriage. It is almost inconceivable today to imagine a time
when mixed-race marriages were banned and anyone today
who still thinks that all marriages should be race pure would
be rightfully labelled an extreme bigot. In fifty years, the
same will likely happen to opponents of gay marriage.

The Supreme Court in *Obergefell* cited *Loving* nearly
a dozen times, basing their decision on the same principle:
everyone deserves equal protection under the law and marriage is one of those protected rights. Justice Samuel Alito
dissented, joined by Antonin Scalia and Clarence Thomas,
stating that Constitution "says nothing about a right to
same-sex marriage." and that same-sex marriage "lacks
deep roots" and "is contrary to long-established tradition."
One wonders how Justices Alito, Scalia, and Thomas (whose
wife is white) would have voted in *Loving*.

History has not been kind to conservatives. In the
1960s, conservatives warned that the creation of the Medi-

care program would lead to socialism and end liberty [page 239]. In the 1930s, conservatives said that Social Security would lead to socialism and end liberty [page 231]. Even before that, they used the same arguments against child labor laws [page 227] and the income tax [page 223]. The same arguments used against the Affordable Care Act today ring hollow. Similarly, what conservatives have said on any major social issue, like slavery, women's suffrage, or child labor, have proven to be wrong. So the question arises: when have conservatives ever been right?

The issue isn't about Democrats versus Republicans. As any political historian knows, party lines between progressivism and conservatism are blurry. There have been conservative Democrats, such as Senator Strom Thurmond from South Carolina, and progressive Republicans, such as Robert La Follette, governor and senator from Wisconsin. To add to the complexity, politicians in history don't fall cleanly into today's liberal or conservative boxes. Republican Theodore Roosevelt was progressive on environmental protection and big business but conservative on immigration policy and Native American rights. Democrat Woodrow Wilson was liberal on international human rights and conservative on gender equality and racial justice. Abraham Lincoln was a Republican.

So what's conservatism? Conservatism is a belief in and a defense of power and the status quo. As the *National Review*, the preeminent conservative journal, explains in its inaugural issue:

> A conservative is someone who stands athwart history, yelling Stop, at a time when no one is inclined to do so, or to have much patience with those who so urge it.
>
> *"Our Mission Statement" in* National Review, *November 19, 1955*

In simple terms, conservatism resists change and wants to maintain the status quo. It is a reaction against liberalism and progressivism, which want to give freedom and equality to those with less power and money. Instead conservatism tries to defend the power of the powerful and the wealth of the wealthy. At its essence, conservatism is a reaction to expanding rights to those who did not have it before. A deep authoritarian impulse is often evident in conservative movements. The adherence to the status quo is not always mere resistance to change but a desire to strengthen and reinforce existing power structures. When conservatives think those hierarchies are under threat, it's not uncommon to meet those (real or imaginary) threats with (real or rhetorical) violence. This ugly reactionary impulse stretches from Jim Crow [pages 67 and 69] to abortion [page 176] to immigration [page 106] and gay marriage [page 153].

This is a history of American conservatism in quotes. Prominent politicians spoke most of these words in public, because at the time they were perfectly acceptable to say on the Congressional record, on the campaign trail, or to the media. As you read them, keep in mind the policies supported by these words denied the safety, freedom, and liberty of millions of Americans. Even today's conservatives would never accept historical conservative positions on issues this country has faced. The needle always moves left.

The United States was founded on the idea that people are equal and endowed with certain unalienable rights. In the long arc of time, we've applied these truths to more and more people. Meanwhile, calls for preserving the prejudices of the status quo inevitably sound odious and shameful. If history is any guide, what conservatives say today will sound racist and bigoted to everyone in the future. The principle of liberty and justice for all is powerful, original, and universal. Why are conservatives always wrong about that?

what have conservatives said about …

Slavery

JAMES H. HAMMOND	1836
JOHN C. CALHOUN	1837
DR. SAMUEL CARTWRIGHT	1851
JEFFERSON DAVIS	1856–1861
SAMUEL F.B. MORSE	1860
ALEXANDER STEPHENS	1863
WOODROW WILSON	1897
LOY MAUCH	2009

J. H. Hammond

Our slaves are a peaceful, kind-hearted and affectionate race; satisfied with their lot, happy in their comforts, and devoted to their masters. It will be no easy thing to seduce them from their fidelity.

1836

Although I am perfectly satisfied that no human process can elevate the black man to an equality with the white—admitting that it could be done—are we prepared for the consequence which then must follow? Are the people of the North prepared to place their political power on an equality with their own? Are we prepared to see them mingling in our legislatures? Is any portion of this country prepared to see them enter these halls and take their seats by our sides, in perfect equality with the white rep- resentatives of an Anglo-Saxon race—to see them fill that chair—to see them placed at the heads of your departments; or to see, perhaps, some Othello, or Toussaint, or Boyer, gifted with genius and inspired by ambition grasp the presidential wreath, and wield the destiny of this great republic? From such a picture I turn with irrepressible disgust.

1836

JAMES H. HAMMOND
Congressman, governor, and senator (SC)

4

Instead of an evil, . . . [slavery is] a positive good. . . the most safe and stable basis for free institutions in the world. . . . I might well challenge a comparison between them and the more direct, simple, and patriarchal mode by which the labor of the African race is, among us, commanded by the European. Compare his condition with the tenants of the poor houses in the more civilized portions of Europe—look at the sick, and the old and infirm slave, on one hand, in the midst of his family and friends, under the kind superintending care of his master and mistress, and compare it with the forlorn and wretched condition of the pauper in the poorhouse.

1837

The two great divisions of society are not the rich and the poor, but white and black, and all the former, the poor as well as the rich, belong to the upper class.

In speech to Congress, 1849

JOHN C. CALHOUN
Senator (SC)

*Union soldiers Jesse L. Berch, left, and Frank M. Rockwell,
right, standing ready to protect the young African American
woman whom they helped escape from slavery*

Drapetomania, or the Disease Causing Negroes to Run Away

It is unknown to our medical authorities, although its diagnostic symptom, the absconding from service, is well known to our planters and overseers. . . . [It] was necessary to have a new term to express it. The cause in the most of cases, . . . is as much a disease of the mind as any other species of mental alienation. . . . With the advantages of proper medical advice, strictly followed, this. . . can be almost entirely prevented. . . .

If the white man attempts to oppose the Deity's will, by trying to make the negro anything else than "the submissive knee-bender," (which the Almighty declared he should be,) . . . ; or if he abuses the power which God has given him over his fellow-man, by being cruel to him, . . . the negro will run away; but if he keeps him in the position that we learn from the Scriptures he was intended to occupy, that is, the position of submission; and if his master or overseer be kind and gracious in his hearing towards him, without condescension, and at the same time ministers to his physical wants, and protects him from abuses, the negro is spell-bound, and cannot run away.

DR. SAMUEL CARTWRIGHT
*"Diseases and Peculiarities of the Negro Race,"
published in* De Bow's Review, *1851*

I Sell the Shadow to Support the Substance.

SOJOURNER TRUTH.

*African-American abolitionist and women's
rights activist, Sojourner Truth, ca. 1864*

Dysaethesia Aethiopica, or Hebetude of Mind and Obtuse Sensibility of Body—A Disease Peculiar to Negroes—Called by Overseers, "Rascality"

Dysaesthesia Aethiopica is a disease peculiar to negroes, affecting both mind and body in a manner. . . From the careless movements of the individuals affected with the complaint, they are apt to do much mischief, which appears as if intentional, but is mostly owing to the stupidness of mind and insensibility of the nerves induced by the disease. Thus, they break, waste and destroy everything they handle, —abuse horses and cattle, —tear, burn or rend their own clothing, and, paying no attention to the rights of property, steal others, to replace what they have destroyed. They wander about at night, and keep in a half nodding sleep during the day. They slight their work, —cut up corn, cane, cotton or tobacco when hoeing it, as if for pure mischief. They raise disturbances with their overseers and fellow-servants without cause or motive, and seem to be insensible to pain when subjected to punishment. . . . The disease is the natural offspring of negro liberty—the liberty to be idle, to wallow in filth, and to indulge in improper food and drinks.

DR. SAMUEL CARTWRIGHT
*"Diseases and Peculiarities of the Negro Race,"
published in* De Bow's Review, *1851*

[Slavery] was established by decree of Almighty God. . . it is sanctioned in the Bible, in both Testaments, from Genesis to Revelation. . . it has existed in all ages, has been found among the people of the highest civilization, and in nations of the highest proficiency in the arts. . . Let the gentleman go to Revelation to learn the decree of God—let him go to the Bible. . . I said that slavery was sanctioned in the Bible, autho-rized, regulated, and recognized from Genesis to Revelation. . . Slavery existed then in the earliest ages, and among the chosen people of God; and in Revelation we are told that it shall exist till the end of time shall come. You find it in the Old and New Testaments—in the prophe-cies, psalms, and the epistles of Paul; you find it recognized, sanctioned everywhere.

1856

We recognize the negro as God and God's Book and God's Laws, in nature, tell us to recognize him—our inferior, fitted expressly for servi-tude. . . You cannot transform the negro into anything one-tenth as useful or as good as what slavery enables them to be.

1861

JEFFERSON DAVIS
*Senator (MS) and future president
of the Confederate States*

11

Are there not in this relation [of master to slave], when faithfully carried out according to Divine directions, some of the most beautiful examples of domestic happiness and contentment that this fallen world knows? Protection and judicious guidance and careful provision on the one part; cheerful obedience, affection and confidence on the other.

SAMUEL F. B. MORSE

Inventor of Morse code and mayoral candidate for New York City, 1863

14

Our new government is founded upon exactly the opposite idea; its foundations are laid, its corner-stone rests, upon the great truth that the negro is not equal to the white man; that slavery subordination to the superior race is his natural and normal condition. This, our new government, is the first, in the history of the world, based upon this great physical, philosophical, and moral truth.

ALEXANDER STEPHENS
*Congressman and governor (GA),
vice president of the Confederate
States, 1861*

The domestic slaves, at any rate, and almost all who were much under the master's eye, were happy and well cared for.

WOODROW WILSON
Future president of the United States, 1897

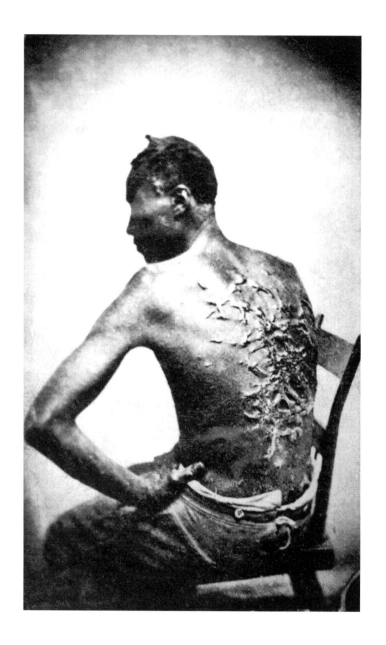

. . . If slavery were so God-awful, why didn't Jesus or Paul condemn it, why was it in the Constitution and why wasn't there a war before 1861? The South has always stood by the Constitution and limited government. When one attacks the Confederate Battle Flag, he is certainly denouncing these principles of government as well as Christianity.

LOY MAUCH

*State representatives (AR), in letter to
the* Democrat-Gazette, *January, 2009*

what have conservatives said about ...

Native Americans

GEORGE WASHINGTON	1779
THOMAS JEFFERSON	1813
JOHN MARSHALL	1823
ANDREW JACKSON	1833
THEODORE ROOSEVELT	1886–1889

The immediate objectives are the total destruction and devastation of their settlements and the capture of as many prisoners of every age and sex as possible. It will be essential to ruin their crops in the ground and prevent their planting more.

GEORGE WASHINGTON

*General and future president of the United States,
in orders to General John Sullivan, May 31, 1779*

This unfortunate race, whom we had been taking so much pains to save and to civilize, have by their unexpected desertion and ferocious barbarities justified extermination and now await our decision on their fate.

THOMAS JEFFERSON
President of the United States,
The Papers of Thomas Jefferson,
December 29, 1813

The tribes of Indians inhabiting this country were fierce savages, whose occupation was war, and whose subsistence was drawn chiefly from the forest. . . That law which regulates, and ought to regulate in general, the relations between the conqueror and conquered was incapable of application to a people under such circumstances. . . Discovery gave an exclusive right to extinguish the Indian title of occupancy, either by purchase or by conquest.

JOHN MARSHALL
*Chief justice presiding in Johnson and
Graham's Lessee v. William M'Intosh, 1823*

They have neither the intelligence, the industry, the moral habits, nor the desire of improvement which are essential to any favorable change in their condition. Established in the midst of another and a superior race, and without appreciating the causes of their inferiority or seeking to control them, they must necessarily yield to the force of circumstances and ere long disappear.

ANDREW JACKSON
*President of the United States,
in his fifth annual message,
December 3, 1833*

I don't go so far as to think that the only good Indians are dead Indians, but I believe nine out of ten are, and I shouldn't like to inquire too closely into the case of the tenth. The most vicious cowboy has more moral principle than the average Indian. Turn three hundred low families of New York into New Jersey, support them for fifty years in vicious idle- ness, and you will have some idea of what the Indians are.

THEODORE ROOSEVELT
Future president of the United States, 1886

The settler and pioneer have at bottom had justice on their side; this great continent could not have been kept as nothing but a game preserve for squalid savages. Moreover, to the most oppressed Indian nations the whites often acted as a protection, or, at least, they deferred instead of hastening their fate.

THEODORE ROOSEVELT
Future president of the United States,
The Winning of the West, *Vol. I., 1889*

what have conservatives said about …

Imperialism and the American Empire

ORVILLE H. PLATT	1899
WORTHINGTON C. FORD	1899
ALBERT BEVERIDGE	1900
HENRY L. WELLS	1900

Filipino casualties on the first day of the
Philippine–American War, February 5, 1899

Why Are
Conservatives
Always Wrong?

IMPERIALISM
AND THE
AMERICAN
EMPIRE

I believe that we have been chosen
to carry forward this great work
of uplifting humanity on earth. . .
The English-speaking people. . . is
charged with this great mission. . .
We propose to proclaim liberty and
justice and the protection of life and
human rights wherever the flag of
the United States is planted.

ORVILLE H. PLATT
Senator (CT), 1899

U.S. soldiers in Manilla, during the
Philippine-American war, ca. 1899

Why Are
Conservatives
Always Wrong?

IMPERIALISM
AND THE
AMERICAN
EMPIRE

Questions of conscience need not trouble us. . . Here are rich lands, held by those who do not or cannot get the best out of them, and awaiting the fructifying application of capital and organization in commerce. Under this beneficent view the natives, an inferior race, must get out or become laborers. The Filipino is an incumbrance to be got rid of, unless he accepts the mandates of a purchasing and a conquering power.

WORTHINGTON C. FORD
*U.S. State Department and
Treasury Department, 1899*

Mr. President, this question is deeper than any question of party politics. . . It is elemental. It is racial. God has not been preparing the English-speaking and Teutonic peoples for a thousand years for nothing but vain and idle self-contemplation and self-admiration. No! He has made us the master organizers of the world to establish system where chaos reigns. He has given its the spirit of progress to overwhelm the forces of reaction throughout the earth. He has made us adepts in government that we may administer government among savage and senile peoples. Were it not for such a force as this the world would relapse into barbarism and night. And of all our race He has marked the American people as His chosen nation to finally lead in the regeneration of the world. This is the divine mission of America, and it holds for us all the profit, all the glory, all the happiness possible to man. We are trustees of the world's progress, guardians of its righteous peace. The judgment of the Master is upon us: "Ye have been faithful over a few things; I will make you ruler over many things."

ALBERT BEVERIDGE
Senator (IN), from Congressional Record, *1900*

*Oregon Volunteer Infantry on firing line outside
of Pasig, Philippine Islands, March 14, 1899*

Why Are
Conservatives
Always Wrong?

IMPERIALISM
AND THE
AMERICAN
EMPIRE

There is no question that our men do "shoot niggers" somewhat in the sporting spirit, but that is because war and their environments have rubbed off the thin veneer of civilization. . . Undoubtedly, they do not regard the shooting of Filipinos just as they would the shooting of white troops. This is partly because they are "only niggers," and partly because they despise them for their treacherous servility. . . The soldiers feel they are fighting with savages, not with soldiers.

HENRY L. WELLS
Journalist, 1900

what have conservatives said about …

Women's Suffrage

WOODROW WILSON 1876

CHARLES CARTER 1915

WILLIAM MULKEY 1915

FRANK CLARK 1915

EDWIN WEBB 1915

STANLEY BOWDLE 1915

THOMAS GIRLING 1917

F. A. DUXBURY 1917

Woodrow Wilson with his wife and daughters, 1912

Universal suffrage is at the foundation of every evil in this country.

WOODROW WILSON
Future president of the United States, 1876

Were it not for shattering an ideal, were it not for dethroning her from that high pedestal upon which we are accustomed to place her, and dragging her down to the level of us beastly men, I believe I might even today be willing to vote for universal woman suffrage.

CHARLES CARTER
Congressman (OK), 1915

The great cry is that woman should be allowed to vote in order to protect themselves. Against what? Do men oppress them? Do we act toward them as though they were not American citizens or entitled to the protection of our laws? On the contrary, we show them every consideration, provide for their safety, and protect their interest always and everywhere. If, therefore, they could vote, they could not improve their condition, but might place themselves in a position that men would not be as tolerant and patient and chivalrous toward them as they are now.

WILLIAM MULKEY
Congressman (AL), 1915

The Word of God inveighs against women suffrage, and the plans of the Creator would be, in a measure, subverted by its adoption. God has decreed that man is to be the head of the family and woman is to be his "helpmeet," and any attempt to change this order of human affairs is an attempt to change and to over- throw one of the solemn decrees of God Almighty.

FRANK CLARK
Congressman (FL), 1915

Mr. Speaker, I am opposed to woman suffrage, but I am not opposed to woman. I am unwilling, as a southern man, to force upon her any burden which will distract this loving potentate from her sacred, God-imposed duties. I am unwilling to force her into the vortex of politics, where her sensitiveness and her modesty will often be offended.

EDWIN WEBB
Congressman (NC), 1915

The women of this smart capitol are beautiful. Their beauty is disturbing to business; their feet are beautiful; their ankles are beautiful, but here I must pause—for they are not interested in the state.

STANLEY BOWDLE
Congressman (OH), 1915

Currier & Ives print speculating what might happen
if women are granted the right to vote, 1869

Women shouldn't be dragged into the dirty pool of politics. . . [It] would cause irreparable damage at great expense to the state.

THOMAS GIRLING
State representative (MN), 1917

Disaster and ruin would overtake the nation. . . [because] men could never resist the blandishments of women. Instead, women should attach themselves to some man who will represent them in public affairs.

F. A. DUXBURY
State senator (MN), 1917

what have conservatives said about …

Jim Crow and Segregation

ROGER B. TANEY	1857
BENJAMIN TILLMAN	1900–1901
JAMES KIMBLE VARDAMAN	1900–1907
WOODROW WILSON	1901–1915
RICHARD RUSSELL	1935–1964
THEODORE BILBO	1938–1947
BURNET R. MAYBANK	1944
EUGENE TALMADGE	1944
ALLEN ELLENDER	1946
STROM THURMOND	1948–1956
GEORGE C. WALLACE	1963–1964

[People of African ancestry] are . . . not included, and were not intended to be included, under the word "citizens" in the Constitution, and can therefore claim none of the rights and privileges which that instrument provides for and secures to citizens of the United States.

ROGER B. TANEY
Chief Justice of the United States speaking for the majority, Dred Scott v. Sandford, 1857

We of the South have never recognized the right of the negro to govern white men, and we never will. We have never believed him to be the equal of the white man, and we will not submit to his gratifying his lust on our wives and daughters without lynching him.

1900

We have done our level best [to prevent blacks from voting]. . . we have scratched our heads to find out how we could eliminate the last one of them. We stuffed ballot boxes. We shot them. We are not ashamed of it.

1900

BENJAMIN TILLMAN
Governor and senator (SC)

President Roosevelt and Booker T. Washington reviewing sixty-one "industry" floats. Tuskegee, AL, January 12, 1906

The action of President Roosevelt in entertaining that nigger [Booker T. Washington] will necessitate our killing a thousand niggers in the South before they will learn their place again.

BENJAMIN TILLMAN
Governor and senator (SC), 1901

There is no use to equivocate or lie about the matter. [The Mississippi Constitutional Convention of 1890] was held for no other purpose than to eliminate the nigger from politics; not the "ignorant and vicious," as some of those apologists would have you believe, but the nigger. . . Let the world know it just as it is.

1900

If it is necessary every Negro in the state will be lynched; it will be done to maintain white supremacy.

1907

JAMES KIMBLE VARDAMAN
Governor and senator (MS)

Meeting of the Ku Klux Klan, 1924

The white men were roused by a mere instinct of self-preservation —until at last there had sprung into existence a great Ku Klux Klan, a veritable empire of the South, to protect the Southern country.

WOODROW WILSON
Future president of the United States, 1901

If the colored people made a mistake in voting for me, they ought to correct it.

1914

Segregation is not a humiliation but a benefit, and ought to be so regarded by you gentlemen.

1915

WOODROW WILSON
President of the United States

If you succeed in the passage of [the federal anti-lynching bill], you will open the floodgates of hell in the South. Raping, mobbing, lynching, race riots, and crime will be increased a thousandfold; and upon your garments and the garments of those who are responsible for the passage of the measure will be the blood of the raped and outraged daughters of Dixie, as well as the blood of the perpetrators of these crimes that the red-blooded Anglo-Saxon White Southern men will not tolerate.

1938

The South stands for blood, for the preservation of the blood of the white race. To preserve her blood, the white South must absolutely deny social equality to the Negro regardless of what his individual accomplishments might be. This is the premise—openly and frankly stated—upon which Southern policy is based. This position is so thoroughly justified in the minds of white Southerners that it is sometimes difficult for them to comprehend the reasoning of those who seriously dispute it.

1947

THEODORE BILBO
Governor and senator (MS)

Senator Richard Russel, third from left

As one who was born and reared in the atmosphere of the Old South, with six generations
of my forebears now resting beneath Southern
soil, I am willing to go as far and make as great a
sacrifice to preserve and insure white supremacy
in the social, economic, and political life of our
state as any man who lives within her borders.

1935

I believe that the Negro is entitled to equal and
exact justice before the law and that he is entitled to every right that I enjoy. There is nothing
in our Constitution, . . . however, that says we
must enjoy these rights together at the same
time and in the same place. . . I cannot believe
that anyone who supports this iniquitous legislation has any real understanding of the extent
to which it destroys the Constitution.

1964

RICHARD RUSSELL
Senator (GA)

**Regardless of the Supreme
Court decision and any laws
that may be passed by Congress, we in South Carolina
are going to do whatever
we can to protect our white
primaries.**

BURNET R. MAYBANK
Senator and governor (SC), 1944

Eugene Talmadge, on right

Wise Negroes will stay away from white folks' ballot boxes. Maybe it would not be inappropriate to warn some of those fellows to be careful. Neither the U.S. Attorneys or Jimmy Carmichael [Talmadge's opponent] will have a corporal's guard to back them up. We are the true friends of the Negroes, always have been, and always will be, so long as they stay in the definite place we have provided for them.

EUGENE TALMADGE
Governor (GA) 1944

I believe in white supremacy, and as long as I am in the Senate I expect to fight for white supremacy.

ALLEN ELLENDER
Senator (LA), 1946

An American should be able
choose to work in a place where
he is with his kind of people and
not find that at the counters, desk
or benches they will be forced to
work, side by side, with all types
of people of all races; that in the
lunchrooms, rest rooms, recreation
rooms, they will be compelled by
law to mingle with persons and
races which all their lives they have
by free choice, avoided in social
and business intercourse.

1948

[Martin Luther] King demeans his
race and retards the advancement
of his people.

date unknown

STROM THURMOND
Senator (SC)

African American boys and girls walking through a crowd of white boys during a period of violence related to school integration. Clinton, TN, December 4, 1956

I wanna tell you, ladies and gentlemen, that there's not enough troops in the army to force the Southern people to break down segregation and admit the nigra [*sic*] race into our theaters, into our swimming pools, into our homes, and into our churches.

STROM THURMOND
*Candidate for the States Rights Democratic Party in
1948 presidential election, future senator (SC), 1948*

[Integrating public schools] is destroying the amicable relations between the white and Negro races that have been created through ninety years of patient effort by the good people of both races. It has planted hatred and suspicion where there has been heretofore friendship and understanding.

STROM THURMOND,
RICHARD RUSSELL
*Senators (SC and GA respectively) and other
Southern legislators in a letter to the Senate, 1956*

*George Wallace attempting to block integration
at the University of Alabama, June 11, 1963*

It is very appropriate that from this cradle of the Confederacy, this very heart of the great Anglo-Saxon Southland, that today we sound the drum for freedom as have our generations of forebears before us time and again down through history. Let us rise to the call for freedom-loving blood that is in us and send our answer to the tyranny that clanks its chains upon the South. In the name of the greatest people that have ever trod this earth, I draw the line in the dust and toss the gauntlet before the feet of tyranny, and I say segregation now, segregation tomorrow and segregation forever!

First inaugural speech as governor (AL), 1963

A racist is one who despises someone because of his color, and an Alabama segregationist is one who conscientiously believes that it is in the best interest of Negro and white to have a separate education and social order.

1964

GEORGE C. WALLACE
Governor (AL)

what have conservatives said about …

Immigration

CALIFORNIA CONSTITUTIONAL CONVENTION	1878
THEODORE ROOSEVELT	1885
JOHN PARKER	1911
WOODROW WILSON	1912
CALVIN COOLIDGE	1921
ELLISON DuRANT SMITH	1924
COMPTON I. WHITE	1943
BRIAN JAMES	2006
DONALD TRUMP	2012–2015
STEVE KING	2013

Chinese musicians performing in the U.S., March 15, 1904

The Chinese bring with them habits and customs the most vicious and demoralizing. They are scornful of our laws and institutions. . . .They are, generally destitute of moral principle. They are incapable of patriotism, and are utterly unfitted for American citizenship.

CALIFORNIA CONSTITUTIONAL CONVENTION
1878

The average Catholic Irish-man of the first generation . . . [is a] low, venal, corrupt, and unintelligent brute.

THEODORE ROOSEVELT

Future president of the United States, 1885

An Italian family who have been in the U.S. only one month.
The mother is learning to make lace for a factory near by, 1911

[Italians are] just a little worse than the Negro, being if any- thing filthier in [their] habits, lawless, and treacherous.

JOHN PARKER
Future governor (LA), 1911

In the matter of Chinese and Japanese coolie immigration, I stand for the national policy of exclusion. We cannot make a homogenous population out of people who do not blend with the Caucasian race. . . Oriental Coolieism will give us another race problem to solve and surely we have had our lesson.

WOODROW WILSON
President of the United States, 1912

There are racial considerations too grave to be brushed aside for any sentimental reasons. Biological laws tell us that certain divergent people will not mix or blend. The Nordics propagate themselves success-fully. With other races, the outcome shows deterioration on both sides. Quality of mind and body suggests that observance of ethnic law is as great a necessity to a nation as immigration law.

CALVIN COOLIDGE
President of the United States, 1921

Immigrant children photographed on Ellis Island, 1908

Thank God we have in America perhaps the largest percentage of any country in the world of the pure, unadulterated Anglo-Saxon stock; certainly the greatest of any nation in the Nordic breed. It is for the preservation of that splendid stock that has characterized us that I would make this not an asylum for the oppressed of all countries, but a country to assimilate and perfect that splendid type of manhood that has made America the foremost Nation in her progress and in her power, and yet the youngest of all the nations.

ELLISON DuRANT SMITH
*Senator (SC), 1924, on closing
the U.S. to immigration*

Chinese-American girl playing hopscotch with friends outside her home in Flatbush. New York City, NY, August 1942

I do not think we can take the Chinese with their habits and mentalities in this year and time into our great American melting pot and in ten years or a hundred years bring them up to our standards of civilization.

COMPTON I. WHITE
Congressman (ID), 1943

What we'll do is randomly pick one night—every week— where we will kill whoever crosses the border. Step over here and you die.

BRIAN JAMES
KFYI conservative radio host, 2006

For everyone who's a valedictorian, there's another 100 out there that weigh 130 pounds and they've got calves the size of cantaloupes because they're hauling 75 pounds of marijuana across the desert.

STEVE KING

*Congressman (IA), on
immigration reform, 2013*

I really believe there's a birth certificate. Why doesn't [Obama] show his birth certificate? And you know what? I wish he would. I think it's a terrible pale [*sic*] that's hanging over him. . . . I want him to show his birth certificate. I want him to show his birth certificate. There's something on that birth certificate that he doesn't like.

2012

The U.S. has become a dumping ground for everybody else's problems. . . . When Mexico sends its people, they're not sending their best. They're not sending you. They're not sending you. They're sending people that have lots of problems, and they're bringing those problems with us. They're bringing drugs. They're bringing crime. They're rapists. And some, I assume, are good people.

2015

DONALD TRUMP
*Republican presidential candidate
during 2016 election*

what have conservatives said about ...

Civil Rights

WILLIAM REHNQUIST	1952
WILLIAM F. BUCKLEY JR.	1957
NATIONAL REVIEW	1960–1965
JESSE HELMS	1963
RONALD REAGAN	1965–1968
LEE ATWATER	1981
EDWIN MEESE	1985
RUSH LIMBAUGH	1990–2007
RON PAUL	1989–1992
WILLIAM BENNETT	2005
ALBERTO GONZALES	2007

I realize that it is an unpopular and unhumanitarian position, for which I have been excoriated by "liberal" colleagues, but I think *Plessy v. Ferguson* [the doctrine of "separate by equal"] was right and should be reaffirmed. To the argument that a majority may not deprive a minority of its constitutional right, the answer must be made that while this is sound in theory, in the long run it is the majority who will determine what the constitutional rights of the minority are.

WILLIAM REHNQUIST
Future chief justice of the United States, 1952

*Rally at Arkansas state capitol protesting the admission of the
"Little Rock Nine" to Central High School, August 20, 1959*

The central question that emerges is whether the White community in the South is entitled to take such measures [including violence], as are necessary to prevail, politically and culturally, in areas in which it does not predominate numerically? The sobering answer is Yes—the White community is so entitled because, for the time being, it is the advanced race.

WILLIAM F. BUCKLEY JR.
Editorial in National Review, *1957*

*Rev. Martin Luther King, center left, with
leaders at the March on Washington, 1963*

We offer the following on the crisis in the Senate and the South: In the Deep South the Negroes are, by comparison with the Whites, retarded ("unadvanced" the National Association for the Advancement of Colored People might put it). . . Leadership in the South, then quite properly rests in White hands. Upon the White population this fact imposes moral obligations of paternalism, patience, protection, devotion, and sacrifice.

1960

There are, to be sure, times when the emotional impulses of an outraged people should indeed crystallize in massive demonstrations. But such situations are very rare indeed. . . Mass demonstrations, in a free society, should be reserved for situations about which there is simply no doubting the correct moral course.

*Editorial against Martin Luther King's
March on Washington, 1963*

NATIONAL REVIEW

The internal order is now in jeopardy; and it is
in jeopardy because of the doings of such high-
minded, self-righteous "children of light" as the
Rev. Dr. Martin Luther King and his associates
in the leadership role of the "civil rights" movement. If you are looking for those ultimately
responsible for the murder, arson, and looting
in Los Angeles, look to them: they are the guilty
ones, these apostles of "non-violence."

NATIONAL REVIEW
Following the Watts Riots in Los Angeles, CA, 1965

Congress of Racial Equality conducts march in memory of the African-American
children killed in the Birmingham, AL bombings. September 22, 1963

The Negro cannot count forever on the kind of restraint that's thus far left him free to clog the streets, disrupt traffic, and interfere with other men's rights.

JESSE HELMS
Senator (NC), on civil rights protests, 1963

I would have voted against the Civil Rights Act of 1964.

1966

It is the sort of great tragedy that began when we began compromising with law and order, and people started choosing which laws they'd break.

On Martin Luther King's assassination, 1968

RONALD REAGAN
*Governor (CA) and future
president of the United States*

*Lee Atwater, third from left, "jams" with President George
H.W. Bush at Inaugural festivity, January 21, 1989*

You start out in 1954 by saying, "Nigger, nigger, nigger." By 1968 you can't say "nigger"—that hurts you, backfires. So you say stuff like forced busing, states' rights, and all that stuff, and you're getting so abstract. Now, you're talking about cutting taxes, and all these things you're talking about are totally economic things and a by-product of them is, blacks get hurt worse than whites. . . . "We want to cut this," is much more abstract than even the busing thing, and a hell of a lot more abstract than "Nigger, nigger."

LEE ATWATER
Reagan campaign strategist, 1981

*Edwin Meese at podium during a White House
press briefing on Iran-Contra, November 25, 1986*

U.S. NEWS: You criticize the Miranda ruling, which gives suspects the right to have a lawyer present before police questioning. Shouldn't people, who may be innocent, have such protection?

MEESE: Suspects who are innocent of a crime should. But the thing is, you don't have many suspects who are innocent of a crime. That's contradictory. If a person is innocent of a crime, then he is not a suspect.

> EDWIN MEESE
> *Attorney general during Reagan Administration, 1985*

Racial violence will fill our cities [because] mostly black welfare recipients will feel justified in stealing from mostly white "haves."

RON PAUL

Congressman (TX) and two time presidential candidate. From newsletter, December 1989

Order was only restored in L.A. when it came time for the blacks to pick up their welfare checks three days after rioting began.

RON PAUL POLITICAL REPORT
1992

I've urged everyone in my family to know how to use a gun in self-defense. For the animals are coming.

RON PAUL

Congressman (TX) and two time presidential candidate. From newsletter, October 1992

Have you ever noticed how all composite pictures of wanted criminals resemble Jesse Jackson?

RUSH LIMBAUGH
Quoted in Newsday *article, 1990*

Look, let me put it to you this way: the NFL all too often looks like a game between the Bloods and the Crips without any weapons. There, I said it.

RUSH LIMBAUGH
From radio broadcast, January 19, 2007

It's true if you wanted to reduce crime, you could—if that were your sole purpose —you could abort every black baby in this country, and your crime rate would go down.

WILLIAM BENNETT
Secretary of education during Reagan administration, 2005

There is no express grant of habeas in the Constitution.

ALBERTO GONZALES

*Attorney general during
George W. Bush administration,
2007*

what have
conservatives
said about …

Freedom
to Marry

ROGER B. TANEY 1857

JAMES R. DOOLITTLE 1863

BUCKNER H. PAYNE 1867

MISSOURI v. JACKSON 1883

JOHN WESLEY SHENK 1948

LEON BAZILE 1967

R. D. McILWAINE 1967

BOB JONES UNIVERSITY 1998

LANNY LITTLEJOHN 1999

REPUBLICAN PARTY PLATFORM 2000–2012

JIMMY SWAGGART 2004

TRENT FRANKS 2011

BEN CARSON 2013

Intermarriages between white persons and negroes or mulattoes were regarded as unnatural and immoral.

ROGER B. TANEY
Chief Justice of the United States,
Dred Scott v. Sandford, *1857*

By the laws of Massachu-
setts intermarriages between
these races are forbidden as
criminal. Why forbidden?
Simply because natural instinct revolts at it as wrong.

JAMES R. DOOLITTLE
Senator (WI), 1863

A man can not commit so great an offense against his race, against the country, against his God, in any other way, as to give his daughter in marriage to a negro—a beast—or to take one of their females for his wife.

BUCKNER H. PAYNE

Writing as Ariel, author of The Negro: What Is His Ethnological Status?, *1867*

[Mixed marriages] cannot possibly have any progeny, and such a fact sufficiently justifies those laws which forbid the intermarriage of blacks and whites.

Missouri v. Jackson, *1883*

*Frederick Douglass with his wife,
Helen Pitts Douglass, seated, right,
and her sister Eva Pitts, standing*

The amalgamation of the races is not only unnatural, but is always productive of deplorable results. The purity of the public morals, the moral and physical development of both races, and the highest advancement of civilization. . . all require that [the races] should be kept distinctly separate, and that connections and alliances so unnatural should be prohibited by positive law and subject to no evasion.

JOHN WESLEY SHENK

California Supreme Court justice dissenting,
Perez v. Lippold, *1948*

Almighty God created the races white, black, yellow, malay and red, and he placed them on separate continents. And but for the interference with his arrangement there would be no cause for such marriages. The fact that he separated the races shows that he did not intend for the races to mix.

LEON BAZILE

Judge (VA), upholding conviction of Mildred and Richard Loving for interracial marriage (later overturned by Supreme Court), 1967

[T]he State's prohibition of interracial marriage. . . stands on the
same footing as the prohibition of
polygamous marriage, or incestu-
ous marriage, or the prescription
of minimum ages at which people
may marry, and the prevention of
the marriage of people who are
mentally incompetent.

R. D. McILWAINE
*Assistant attorney general (VA), arguing
for Virginia's ban on interracial marriage
in* Loving v. Virginia, *1967*

Although there is no verse in the Bible that dogmatically says that races should not intermarry, the whole plan of God as He has dealt with the races down through the ages indicates that interracial marriage is not best for man.

JONATHAN PAIT

Community Relations Coordinator for Bob Jones University responding to an admissions inquiry letter, 1998

[Interracial marriage] is not what God intended when he separated the races back in the Babylonian days. The races would be a lot better off if they stuck with their own kind.

LANNY LITTLEJOHN
State representative (SC), 1999

A mother's expression of love for her daughter
and daughter-in-law on their wedding day

We support the traditional definition of "marriage" as the legal union of one man and one woman, and we believe that federal judges and bureaucrats should not force states to recognize other living arrangements as marriages. We do not believe sexual preference should be given special legal protection or standing in law.

*Adopted at GOP National Convention,
August 12, 2000*

We strongly support a Constitutional amendment that fully protects marriage, and we [oppose] forcing states to recognize other living arrangements as equivalent to marriage. The well-being of children is best accomplished [when] nurtured by their mother and father anchored by the bonds of marriage. We believe that legal recognition and the accompanying benefits afforded couples should be preserved for that unique and special union of one man and one woman which has historically been called marriage.

September 1, 2004

REPUBLICAN PARTY PLATFORM

Marriage Equality Rally at the U.S. Supreme Court, Washington, D.C., March 26, 2013

I've never seen a man in my life I wanted to marry. And I'm going to be blunt and plain: If one ever looks at me like that, I'm going to kill him and tell God he died.

REV. JIMMY SWAGGART

Pastor, author and televangelist, 2004

Newly married couples leaving City Hall in Seattle are greeted by well-wishers on the first day of same-sex marriage in Washington state, December 9, 2012

It not only is a complete undermining of the principles of family and marriage and the hope of future generations, but it completely begins to see our society break down to the extent that that foundational unit of the family that is the hope of survival of this country is diminished to the extent that it literally is a threat to the nation's survival in the long run.

TRENT FRANKS
Congressman (AZ), 2011

A supporter of marriage equality waving the LGBTQ rainbow flag on opening day of arguments at the United States Supreme Court for same-sex marriage, April 28, 2015

We reaffirm our support for a Constitutional amendment defining marriage as the union of one man and one woman.

REPUBLICAN PARTY PLATFORM
August 27, 2012

Marriage Equality Rally at the U.S. Supreme Court, Washington, D.C., March 26, 2013

Marriage is between a man and a
woman. No group, be they gays,
be they pedophiles, be they people
who believe in bestiality, it doesn't
matter what they are. They don't
get to change the definition.

BEN CARSON

*Republican presidential candidate
during 2016 election and Fox News
contributor, 2013*

what have conservatives said about ...

Sexual
Privacy

THOMAS BLILEY	1981
JERRY FALWELLL	1981–1997
THOMAS BLILEY	1981
PATRICK BUCHANAN	1983
WILLIAM F. BUCKLEY JR.	1986
LAWRENCE LOCKMAN	1987
LOUIS FARRAKHAN	1993
JESSE HELMS	1995
FAMILY RESEARCH COUNCIL	2002
REPUBLICAN PARTY PLATFORM	2004

[Decriminalizing sodomy and adultery in the District of Columbia would] legitimize, almost any sexual act or practice between two, or more, people as long as they all agreed to it. . . . by specifically legalizing unusual sexual practices, would condone them. The moral and ethical traditions of this Nation do not condone acts. . . and I do not believe that the people of America believe that they are acceptable and should be allowed by law in the Nation's Capitol.

THOMAS BLILEY
Congressman (VA), 1981

The homosexuals are on the march in this country. Please remember, homosexuals do not reproduce! They recruit! And, many of them are after my children and your children.

1981

AIDS is the wrath of a just God against homosexuals. To oppose it would be like an Israelite jumping in the Red Sea to save one of Pharaoh's charioteers. AIDS is not just God's punishment for homosexuals; it is God's punishment for the society that tolerates homosexuals.

1993

REV. JERRY FALWELL
Evangelical pastor, televangelist and conservative political commentator

If we do not act now, homosexuals will "own" America. If you and I do not speak up now, this homosexual steamroller will literally crush all decent men, women, and children. . . and our nation will pay a terrible price.

REV. JERRY FALWELL

*Evangelical pastor, televangelist and
conservative political commentator, 1997*

[Through AIDS], the sexual revolution has begun to devour its children. And among the revolutionary vanguard, as Gay rights activists, the mortality rate is highest and climbing. . . . The poor homosexuals—they have declared war upon nature, and now nature is exacting an awful retribution.

PATRICK BUCHANAN
*Senior advisor during Nixon and
Reagan administrations, 1983*

Everyone detected with AIDS should be tattooed in the upper forearm, to protect common-needle users, and on the buttocks, to prevent the victimization of other homosexuals.

WILLIAM F. BUCKLEY JR.
1986

In the overwhelming majority of cases, people are dying because of their addiction to sodomy. . . . They are dying because progressive, enlightened, tolerant people in politics and in medicine have assured the public that the practice of sodomy is a legitimate alternative lifestyle, rather than a perverted, depraved crime against humanity.

LAWRENCE LOCKMAN
State representative (ME), 1987

We must change homosexual behavior and get rid of the circum-stances that bring it about.

LOUIS FARRAKHAN
1993

[The government should spend less money on people with AIDS because they got sick as a result of] deliberate, disgusting, revolting conduct.

JESSE HELMS
Senator (NC), 1995

A little-reported fact is that homosexual and lesbian relationships are
far more violent than are traditional
married households.

FAMILY RESEARCH COUNCIL PUBLICATION
*Conservative Christian group and lobbying
organization formed by James Dobson, 2002*

We affirm traditional military culture,
and we affirm that homosexuality is
incompatible with military service.

REPUBLICAN PARTY PLATFORM
September 7, 2004

what have conservatives said about ...

Women's Bodies and Rights

RUSH LIMBAUGH	1987
CLAYTON WILLIAMS	1990
LAWRENCE LOCKMAN	1990
PAT ROBERTSON	1992
DICK ARMEY	1994
TODD AKIN	2012
RICK SANTORUM	2012
RICHARD MOURDOCK	2012

Feminism was established to allow unattractive women easier access to the mainstream.

RUSH LIMBAUGH

Radio talk show host, writer, and conservative political commentator, 1987

Why Are
Conservatives
Always Wrong?

**WOMEN'S
BODIES AND
RIGHTS**

Rape is kinda like the weather. If it's inevitable, relax and enjoy it.

CLAYTON WILLIAMS

Republican nominee for governor (TX), 1990

If a woman has [the right to an abortion], why shouldn't a man be free to use his superior strength to force himself on a woman?. . . At least the rapist's pursuit of sexual freedom doesn't [in most cases] result in anyone's death.

LAWRENCE LOCKMAN
State representative (ME), 1990

Why Are
Conservatives
Always Wrong?

WOMEN'S
BODIES AND
RIGHTS

The feminist agenda is not about equal rights for women. It is about a socialist, anti-family political movement that encourages women to leave their husbands, kill their children, practice witchcraft, destroy capitalism, and become lesbians.

REV. PAT ROBERTSON
Former communications director during Reagan administration, 1992

I am outraged that [the abortion issue] is viewed through the perspective of the woman—a femme-centric perspective that condones the self-indulgent conduct of the woman who was damn careless in the first place.

DICK ARMEY
Congressional majority leader (TX), 1994

Why Are
Conservatives
Always Wrong?

**WOMEN'S
BODIES AND
RIGHTS**

If it's a legitimate rape, the female body has ways to shut that thing down.

TODD AKIN
Congressman (MO), 2012

Why Are
Conservatives
Always Wrong?

WOMEN'S
BODIES AND
RIGHTS

Rape victims should make the best of a bad situation. I believe and I think the right approach is to accept this horribly created—in the sense of rape—but nevertheless a gift in a very broken way, the gift of human life, and accept what God has given to you.

RICK SANTORUM
Senator (PA), 2012

Why Are
Conservatives
Always Wrong?

WOMEN'S
BODIES AND
RIGHTS

Even when life begins in that horrible situation of rape, that it is something that God intended to happen.

RICHARD MOURDOCK

*Republican candidate for
United States Senate (ID), 2012*

Richard
Nixon

A SPECIAL SECTION

RICHARD NIXON   1970–1977

Why Are
Conservatives
Always Wrong?

SPECIAL
SECTION ON
RICHARD
NIXON

Publicly, we say one thing. . . .
Actually, we do another.

1970

I'm not for women, frankly, in
any job. I don't want any of them
around. Thank God we don't have
any in the Cabinet.

September 19, 1971

The Jews are irreligious, atheistic,
immoral bunch of bastards.

February 1, 1972

I am not a crook.

November 17, 1973

When the president does it, that
means it's not illegal.

In interview with David Frost, 1977

RICHARD NIXON
President of the United States

189

*President Nixon, during the broadcast address to the Nation
in which he announced his resignation, April 29, 1974*

Why Are
Conservatives
Always Wrong?

SPECIAL
SECTION ON
RICHARD
NIXON

The White House has no involvement whatever in this particular incident.

RICHARD NIXON
*President of the United States,
June 22, 1972*

what have conservatives said about ...

Religion and Government

JERRY FALWELL	1976
PAT ROBERTSON	1983
TOM DELAY	1999
GLENN BECK	2006
TEXAS REPUBLICAN PARTY PLATFORM	2006

The idea that religion and politics don't mix was invented by the Devil to keep Christians from running their own country.

REV. JERRY FALWELL

Evangelical pastor, televangelist and conservative political commentator, 1976

There is no such thing as separation of church and state in the Constitution. It is a lie of the left and we are not going to take it any more.

REV. PAT ROBERTSON

*Communications director during
Reagan administration, 1993*

Sunday morning in Dayton, TN, where the famous Scopes trial (Tennessee v. John Thomas Scopes) *was held in 1925*

Our school systems teach our children that they are nothing but glorified apes who have evolutionized out of some primordial soup of mud, by teaching evolution as fact.

TOM DELAY

Congressman (TX) and Republican House Whip, saying the underlying cause of the Columbine High School shootings was the teaching of evolution, 1999

Sir, prove to me that you are not working with our enemies.

GLENN BECK

To Congressman Keith Ellison (MN), the first Muslim ever elected to Congress, statement made during the CNN news-commentary program, Glenn Beck, 2006

Our Party pledges to do everything within its power to dispel the myth of separation of church and state.

TEXAS REPUBLICAN PARTY PLATFORM
2006

what have conservatives said about …

War

RONALD REAGAN	1983
TOM DELAY	1988-2003
GEORGE W. BUSH	2000-2003
ARI FLEISCHER	2002
COLIN POWELL	2003
DONALD RUMSFELD	2003-2004
DICK CHENEY	2003-2007
DANA PERRINO	2009
MARY MATALIN	2009
RUDOLPH GIULIANI	2010

The defense policy of the United States is based on a simple premise: The United States does not start fights. We will never be an aggressor. We maintain our strength in order to deter and defend against aggression—to preserve freedom and peace.

RONALD REAGAN
President of the United States, 1983

173 Airborne Brigade in a firefight on
Hill 823 during the Vietnam War

So many minority youths had volunteered. . . that there was literally no room for patriotic folks like [myself].

*Republican House Whip, in response to query
of why he had not served in Vietnam, 1988*

Nothing is more important in the face of a war than cutting taxes.

From a speech made to bankers, March 12, 2003

TOM DELAY

*Congressman (TX) and former
Republican House Majority Leader*

If we're an arrogant nation, they'll resent us; if we're a humble nation, but strong, they'll welcome us. And our nation stands alone right now in the world in terms of power, and that's why we've got to be humble, and yet project strength in a way that promotes freedom.

During presidential debate, 2000

We are doing everything we can to avoid war in Iraq.

2003

GEORGE W. BUSH
President of the United States

The President of the United States and the Secretary of Defense would not assert plainly and bluntly as they have that Iraq has weapons of mass destruction if it was not true.

ARI FLEISCHER
White House press secretary, 2002

There can be no doubt that Saddam Hussein has biological weapons and the capability to rapidly produce more, many more.

COLIN POWELL

*Secretary of state, address to the United Nations
Security Council, February 5, 2003*

*U.S. soldiers righting an armored vehicle after
surviving a buried IED blast, April 15, 2007*

Major combat operations in Iraq have ended.

GEORGE W. BUSH

President of the United States, May 1, 2003

We know where [Iraq's WMD] are. They're in the area around Tikrit and Bagh-dad and east, west, south, and north somewhat.

2003

I can't tell you if the use of force in Iraq today would last five days, or five weeks, or five months, but it cer-tainly isn't going to last any longer than that.

2004

DONALD RUMSFELD
*Secretary of defense during
George W. Bush administration*

We will, in fact, be greeted as lib-
erators. I think it will go relatively
quickly. . . weeks rather than months.

2003

We haven't really had the time yet
to pore through all those records in
Baghdad. We'll find ample evidence
confirming the link, that is the con-
nection if you will between al Qaida
and the Iraqi intelligence services.
They have worked together on a
number of occasions.

2004

DICK CHENEY
Vice president of the United States

The bottom line is that we've had enormous successes [in Iraq] and we will continue to have enormous successes.

DICK CHENEY
Vice president of the United States, 2007

Ground Zero, New York City, NY, September 17, 2001

We did not have a terrorist attack on our country during President Bush's term.

DANA PERRINO

*White House communications director during
George W. Bush administration, 2009*

President Bush inherited the most tragic attack on our own soil in our nation's history.

MARY MATALIN

Counselor to Vice President Dick Cheney, 2009

We had no domestic attacks under Bush.

RUDOLPH GIULIANI

Former mayor of New York City, 2010

what have conservatives said about ...

Economic Regulation

DAVID HILL	1894
GEORGE F. EDMUNDS	1895
WELDON HEYBURN	1908
CLARENCE E. MARTIN	1933
EWIN L. DAVIS	1935
ALF LANDON	1936
EDWARD COX	1938
THE NATIONAL ASSOCIATION OF MANUFACTURERS	1938
RONALD REAGAN	1961–1980
ALAN GREENSPAN	1963–2004
CARL CURTIS	1965
TOM DELAY	1996
PHIL GRAMM	2001
SCOTT WALKER	2015

George F. Edmunds

Why Are
Conservatives
Always Wrong?

ECONOMIC
REGULATION

[If the income tax is passed], it may be impracticable that our distinctively American experiment of individual freedom should go on.

DAVID HILL
Senator (NY), 1894

[The Court must] bring the Congress back to a true sense of the limitations of its powers. . . . [such a tax on wealth will lead to] communism, anarchy, and then, the ever following despotism.

GEORGE F. EDMUNDS
Former senator (VT), 1895

Addie Card, twelve years old, a spinner in the
North Pownal Cotton Mill, VT, February 1910

[If child labor is banned], the child will become a very dominant factor in the household and might refuse perhaps to do chores before six a.m. or after seven p.m. or to perform any labor.

WELDON HEYBURN
Senator (ID), 1908

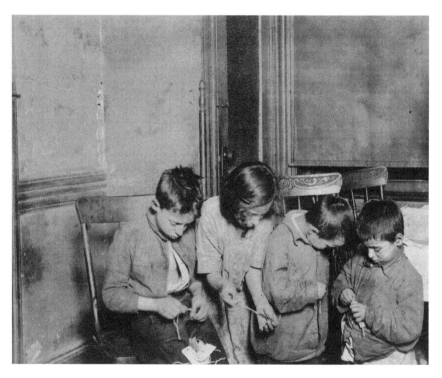

Of a family of seven children, all but two work stringing tags. The oldest child is twelve years old. Newark, NJ, 1923

[Child labor laws are] a communistic effort to nationalize children, making them primarily responsible to him and the government instead of to their parents. It strikes at the home. It appears to be a definite positive plan to destroy the Republic and substitute a social democracy.

CLARENCE E. MARTIN
President of American Bar Association, 1933

[Establishing the Food and Drug Administration] would make it practically impossible for any publisher in the United States to accept any food, drug, or cosmetic advertising without facing squarely into the doors of a jail.

EWIN L. DAVIS
Federal Trade Commission chairperson, 1935

Oklahoma migratory workers washing in a hot spring in the desert. Imperial Valley, CA, March 1937

[The passage of Social Security will open the door to a government power] so vast, so powerful as to threaten the integrity of our institutions and to pull the pillars of the temple down upon the heads of our descendants.

JAMES W. WADSWORTH
Congressman (NY), 1935

Never in the history of the world has any measure been brought here so insidiously designed as to prevent business recovery, to enslave workers and to prevent any possibility of the employers providing work for the people.

JOHN TABER
Congressman (NY), 1935

The lash of the dictator will be felt, . . . and 25 million free American citizens will for the first time submit themselves to a fingerprint test.

DANIEL REED
Congressman (NY), 1935

Alf Landon, facing a battery of cameras when he arrived at the White House for a conference with President Roosevelt

This is the largest tax bill in history. And to call it "social security" is a fraud on the workingman. . . . I am not exaggerating the folly of this legislation. The saving it forces on our workers is a cruel hoax.

ALF LANDON
Governor (KS) and Republican
presidential candidate, 1936

[The Fair Labor Standards Act] will destroy small industry. . . . [these ideas are] the product of those whose thinking is rooted in an alien philosophy and who are bent upon the destruction of our whole constitutional system and the setting up of a red-labor communistic despotism upon the ruins of our Christian civilization.

EDWARD COX
Congressman (GA), 1938

*Billboard on U.S. Highway 99 in California, part of a
nationwide advertising campaign sponsored by the
National Association of Manufacturers, March 1937*

[The Fair Labor Standards Act] constitutes a step in the direction of communism, bolshevism, fascism, and Nazism.

THE NATIONAL ASSOCIATION
OF MANUFACTURERS

1938

*Ronald and Nancy Reagan at the victory celebration
for California Governor, November 8, 1966*

If you don't [write your senator in opposition to Medicare], this program, I promise you, will pass just as surely as the sun will come up tomorrow, and behind it will come other federal programs that will invade every area of freedom as we have known it in this country until one day. . . we will wake to find that we have social- ism. And if you don't do this and I don't do this, one of these days we are going to spend our sunset years telling our children and our chil- dren's children, what it once was like in America when men were free.

RONALD REAGAN
Future governor of California and president of the United States, from an AMA recording "Ronald Reagan Speaks Out Against Socialized Medicine," 1961

[Medicare] is socialism. It moves the country in a direction which is not good for anyone, whether they be young or old. It charts a course from which there will be no turning back.

CARL CURTIS
Senator (NE), 1965

Alan Greenspan, center, testifying before the House Senate
Economic Committee, Washington, D.C. January 6, 1975

[It is a] collectivist [myth that business people]
would attempt to sell unsafe food and drugs,
fraudulent securities, and shoddy buildings. . . .
It is in the self-interest of every businessman
to have a reputation for honest dealings and a
quality product.

1963

Capitalism is based on self-interest and self-
esteem; it holds integrity and trustworthiness
as cardinal virtues and makes them pay off in
the marketplace, thus demanding that men
survive by means of virtue, not vices. It is this
superlatively moral system that the welfare
statists propose to improve upon by means of
preventative law, snooping bureaucrats, and
the chronic goad of fear.

1963

ALAN GREENSPAN
Future chairman of the Federal Reserve

She has eighty names, thirty addresses, twelve Social Security cards and is collecting veteran's benefits on four non-existing deceased husbands. And she is collecting Social Security on her cards. She's got Medicaid, getting food stamps, and she is collecting welfare under each of her names.

On "welfare queens," which was later found to be fictional, 1976

The minimum wage has caused more misery and unemployment than anything since the Great Depression.

1980

RONALD REAGAN
Governor (CA) and president of the United States

Emotional appeals about working families trying to get by on $4.25 an hour are hard to resist. Fortunately, such families don't really exist.

TOM DELAY

Senator (TX) and Republican House Whip, Congressional Record, *1996*

The left claims they're for American workers, and they've just got really lame ideas. Things like the minimum wage.

SCOTT WALKER

Governor (WI) and presidential candidate during 2016 election, 2015

Alan Greenspan

Some people look at subprime lending and see evil. I look at subprime lending and I see the American dream in action.

PHIL GRAMM
Senator (TX), 2001

While local economies may experience significant price imbalances, a national severe price distortion [in the housing market] seems most unlikely in the United States, given its size and diversity.

ALAN GREENSPAN
*Chairman of the Federal Reserve,
October 19, 2004*

what have conservatives said about ...

Science and
the Environment

E. W. TINKER	1947
RONALD REAGAN	1966–1981
JOHN L. KIMBERLEY	1970
LEE IACOCCA	1971
THE NATIONAL ASSOCIATION OF MANUFACTURERS	1987
DONALD R. LYNAM	1984
TOM DELAY	1990
BOB DOLE	1996
DICK CHENEY	2001
JAMES INHOFE	2006
MICHELE BACHMANN	2009
JEFF SESSIONS	2012

Harshaw Chemical Company discharges industrial waste water into the Cuyahoga River, May 1973

Why Are
Conservatives
Always Wrong?

SCIENCE
AND THE
ENVIRONMENT

Experience has also shown that there is another aspect of the problem which, by exciting hasty and improvident legislation, delays progress. I refer to the unpleasant connotation which surrounds the word "pollution." The public is likely to think of that word in terms of sewage and epidemics. I am told, however, that industrial waste is not a menace to public health. . . it is sewage which does the harm.

E. W. TINKER

Executive secretary of the American Paper and Pulp Association, Testimony, Subcommittee of the Committee on Public Works, on the Water Pollution Control Act, 1947

Why Are
Conservatives
Always Wrong?

SCIENCE
AND THE
ENVIRONMENT

A tree is a tree. How many more do you have to look at?

RONALD REAGAN

Opposing expansion of Redwood National Park as governor of California, 1966

Why Are
Conservatives
Always Wrong?

SCIENCE
AND THE
ENVIRONMENT

Trees cause more pollution than automobiles do.

RONALD REAGAN
President of the United States, 1981

Lee Iacocca

Why Are
Conservatives
Always Wrong?

SCIENCE
AND THE
ENVIRONMENT

[Shoulder belts and headrests are] complete wastes of money. . . . We are on a downhill slide the likes of which we have never seen in our business.

LEE IACOCCA
Ford Motor Company, 1971

The [anti-acid rain emissions program's] effects include serious long-term losses in domestic output and employment, heavy cost burdens on manufacturing industries, and a resultant gradual contraction of the entire industrial base. The irony of this bleak scenario is that these economic hardships are borne with no real assurance they would be balanced by a cleaner, healthier environment.

THE NATIONAL ASSOCIATION
OF MANUFACTURERS
1987

There is no evidence that lead in the atmosphere, from autos or any other source, poses a health hazard.

JOHN L. KIMBERLEY

*Executive director of the Lead Industries Association,
Testimony, New York City Council's Committee on
Environmental Protection, 1970*

Why Are
Conservatives
Always Wrong?

SCIENCE
AND THE
ENVIRONMENT

Unfortunately, the atmosphere we're now in prohibits objective scientists from coming forward. And why should they, when they would be crucified by the press, the E.P.A. and the environmentalists? . . . Our stance has been that lead from gasoline does not and has not caused health problems, and I have not seen any data that convinces me differently.

DONALD R. LYNAM
Director of air conservation at the Ethyl Corporation, 1984

It's never been proven that air toxics [*sic*] are hazardous to people.

TOM DELAY

Congressman (TX) and Republican House Whip, 1990

Why Are
Conservatives
Always Wrong?

SCIENCE
AND THE
ENVIRONMENT

We know smoking tobacco is not good for kids, but a lot of other things aren't good. Drinking's not good. Some would say milk's not good.

ROBERT DOLE

*Congressman and senator (KS), and
Republican presidential nominee for
1996 presidential election, 1996*

Why Are
Conservatives
Always Wrong?

SCIENCE
AND THE
ENVIRONMENT

Conservation may be a sign of personal virtue, but it is not a sufficient basis for a sound, comprehensive energy policy.

DICK CHENEY

Vice president of the United States, 2001

Why Are
Conservatives
Always Wrong?

SCIENCE
AND THE
ENVIRONMENT

To my knowledge, nobody has
uttered the term "global warming"
since 2009. It's been completely
refuted in most areas. . . . Those
people who really believe that the
world's coming to an end because
of global warming and that's all
due to man-made, anthropogenic gases, we call those people
alarmists. . . . I really believe it's the
greatest hoax ever perpetrated on
the American people.

JAMES INHOFE
Senator (OK) and chairperson of the
United States Senate Committee on
Environment and Public Works, 2006

Why Are
Conservatives
Always Wrong?

SCIENCE
AND THE
ENVIRONMENT

Carbon dioxide is portrayed as harmful. But there isn't even one study that can be produced that shows that carbon dioxide is a harmful gas.

MICHELE BACHMANN

Congresswoman (MN) and candidate for 2012 Republican presidential nomination, 2009

Why Are
Conservatives
Always Wrong?

SCIENCE
AND THE
ENVIRONMENT

SESSIONS: Madam Chairman, I am offended by that, I'm offended by that—I didn't say anything about the scientists. I said the data shows [sic] it is not warming to the degree that a lot of people predicted, not close to that much. . .

BOXER: The conclusion that you're coming to is shared by 1–2 percent of the scientists. You shouldn't be offended by that. That's the fact.

SESSIONS: I don't believe that's correct.

JEFF SESSIONS
Senator (AL) was surprised when informed by Sen. Barbara Boxer that roughly 98 percent of climate scientists accepted that anthropogenic warming was real and serious, 2012

Early in 2012, the National Weather Service reported 2011 was Texas' driest year on record as well as its second hottest to date. The drought dried up much of Central Texas' water ways. This boat was left to sit in the middle of what is normally a branch of Lake Travis, part of the Colorado River. July 17, 2011

Why Are
Conservatives
Always Wrong?

SCIENCE
AND THE
ENVIRONMENT

ALABAMA

Sen. Richard Shelby (R-AL): "Global warming continues to be an issue of significant debate in Congress and throughout the scientific community. In addition, important scientific research is ongoing as there are still many questions that must be answered before we take steps to address this issue. For example, is the climate change phenomenon cyclical or is it a function of manmade pollutants, or both? I believe the science must be firmly grounded before we take any actions that could seriously cripple many sectors of our economy." [*Shelby Letter*, 12/14/07]

ALASKA

Rep. Don Young (R-AK-At Large): "I think this is the biggest scam since the Teapot Dome." [KTVA Interview, 2/18/10]

Sen. Dan Sullivan (R-AK): "With 7 billion humans on earth, there is likely some impact on nature. The last few years clearly show, though, that there is no concrete scientific consensus on the extent to which humans contribute to climate change." [Newsminer.com, 8/18/14]

ARIZONA

Rep. Trent Franks (R-AZ-08): "While I am concerned about the potential effects of global warming, I have yet to see clear and convincing evidence that it exists beyond historical fluctuations." [AZ Central Candidate Survey, 2008]

Sen. Jeff Flake (R-AZ): "Certainly, nobody can deny that we've had several years of warmer temperatures. If that signals just a routine change that is manmade or not, I don't think anybody can say definitely." [Arizona Public Radio, 10/25/12]

ARKANSAS

Sen. John Boozman (R-AR): "Well I think that we've got perhaps climate change going on. The question is what's causing it. Is man causing it, or, you know, is this a cycle that happens throughout the years, throughout the ages. And you can look back some of the previous times when there was no industrialization, you had these different ages, ice ages, and things warming and things. That's the question." More recently, Sen. Boozman said, "Now I'm not a scientist but I'm an optometrist, and I spent much of my life working with the scientific community. I was a zoology major. And I've said before that there's nothing scientific about discrediting people who present conflicting evidence and ask reasonable questions." [ThinkProgress, 9/13/10; Arkansas Times, 6/21/14]

CALIFORNIA

Rep. Darrell Issa (R-CA-49): "One of the difficulties in examining the issue of the climate change and greenhouse gases is that there is a wide range of scientific opinion on this issue and the science community does not agree to the extent of the problem or the critical threshold of when this problem is truly catastrophic." [Project Vote Smart Issue Position, 1/1/12]

Rep. Doug LaMalfa (R-CA-01): "The climate of the globe has been fluctuating since God created it." [Redding Record, 9/24/14]

Rep. Dana Rohrabacher (R-CA-48): "Just so you'll know, global warming is a total fraud and it's being designed because what you've got is you've got liberals who get elected at the local level want state government to do the work and let them make the decisions. Then, at the state level, they want the federal government to do it. And at the federal government, they want to create global government to control all of our lives." [Huffington Post, 8/12/13]

COLORADO

Rep. Ken Buck (R-CO-04): "Sen. Inhofe was the first person to stand up and say this global warming is the greatest hoax that has been perpetrated. The evidence just keeps supporting his view, and more and more people's view, of what's going on." [ThinkProgress, 8/8/13]

FLORIDA

Rep. Mario Diaz-Balart (R-FL-25): "I know there's a lot of money to be made on the bandwagon of global warming, you can make movies, documentaries, get a lot of research money—and that's okay, I love capitalism. . . My fear is using the bandwagon of global warming to have Congress act on some knee-jerk reaction which will please some editorialists, will hurt our economy, will not do anything to help us in the future." [Mario Diaz-Balart Video, 9/25/07]

Rep. Jeff Miller (R-FL-01): "I have scientists that I rely on, the scientists that I rely on say our climate has changed. It wasn't just a few years ago, what was the problem that existed? It wasn't global warming, we were gonna all be an ice cube. We're not ice cubes. Our climate will continue to change because of the way God formed the earth." According to BuzzFeed, earlier at the same event, Miller announced his intentions to defund the Environmental Protection Agency and responded to questions about a scientific consensus on climate change by saying none existed. [BuzzFeed, 8/14/13]

Sen. Marco Rubio (R-FL): "I do not believe that human activity is causing these dramatic changes to our climate the way these scientists are portraying. And I do not believe that the laws that they propose we pass will do anything about it. Except it will destroy our economy." [Miami Herald Blog, 5/11/14]

GEORGIA

Rep. Tom Price (R-GA-06): "This decision goes against all common sense, especially considering the many recent revelations of errors and obfuscation in the allegedly 'settled science' of global warming." [Republican Study Committee]

IDAHO

Sen. Mike Crapo (R-ID): "While there is no dispute over the fact that the Earth's climate has changed many times over the planet's history, the underlying cause of these climactic shifts is ultimately not well-understood and is a matter of vigorous debate." [Crapo Website]

ILLINOIS

Rep. Rodney Davis (R-IL-13): During an interview with Illinois Public Media radio, a constituent asked Representative Rodney Davis what he planned to do to combat climate change, and he responded that "global warming has stopped 16 years ago." [Illinois Public Media, 10/16/12]

Rep. John Shimkus (R-IL-15): "The earth will end only when God declares it is time to be over. Man will not destroy this earth. This earth will not be destroyed by a flood." [House Subcommittee on Energy and Environment Hearing, 3/25/2009]

INDIANA

Rep. Larry Bucshon (R-IN-08): "It's not about affecting the global temperature and climate change. There's public comments out there that that question has been answered saying 'no. . .' Of all the climatologists whose career depends on the climate changing to keep themselves publishing articles, yes I could read that. But I don't believe it." [The Daily Show, 9/22/14]

IOWA

Rep. Rod Blum (R-IA-01): "Well, it's interesting. I can see why the average citizen is skeptical about this. I guess you can put me in that camp. I'm skeptical. . . I'm not a scientist, and I know most scientists' paychecks come from the federal government, and so right away that makes me a bit skeptical. Thirty years ago we were going into a global cooling period. That makes me skeptical." [Iowa Public Radio, 5/29/14]

KANSAS

Sen. Pat Roberts (R-KS): "There's no question there's some global warming, but I'm not sure what it means. A lot of this is condescending elitism." [Topeka Capital-Journal, 8/24/10]

Why Are
Conservatives
Always Wrong?

SCIENCE
AND THE
ENVIRONMENT

KENTUCKY

Rep. Ed Whitfield (R-KY-01): "Misrepresenting scientific research to support one's own personal beliefs, particularly on an international stage, is dangerous, disingenuous and simply unacceptable. I call on Mr. [Al] Gore to come clean about the real science surrounding climate change and let the American people come to their own conclusions on global warming." [Whitfield Website, 12/15/09]

Sen. Mitch McConnell (R-KY): "For everybody who thinks it's warming, I can find somebody who thinks it isn't." More recently, when asked whether he agreed that human activity was driving climate change, McConnell responded, "I'm not a scientist." [Cincinnati Inquirer, 3/7/14; ThinkProgress, 10/3/14]

LOUISIANA

Sen. David Vitter (R-LA): "I do not think the science clearly supports global warming theory." [KLFY, 10/28/10]

MAINE

Rep. Bruce Poliquin (R-ME-02): "Clearly our climate is changing; the question is, is man responsible for that climate change? I personally am suspect." [Maine Public Broadcasting Network, 6/4/10]

MARYLAND

Rep. Andy Harris (R-MD-01): "I believe the actual science is uncertain. . . We have to understand why it hasn't; before we spend literally, worldwide, trillions of dollars on this, we should understand exactly what's happening, and even more importantly, whether . . . by spending that money, we have a change of affecting it in any significant way. Because I don't believe we are going to convince the rest of the countries of the world not to use more energy.'" [*Star Democrat*, 8/23/13]

MICHIGAN

Rep. Bill Huizenga (R-MI-02): "Today's global warming doomsayers simply lack the scientific evidence to support their claims. A host of leaders in the scientific community have recognized that the argument for drastic anthropogenic global warming is no longer based on science, but is being driven by irrational fanaticism." [VoteMI.org]

MINNESOTA

Rep. Tom Emmer (R-MN-06): "Biodiversity, diversity to me means you've got to look at both sides. You know what, the empirical evidence does not support this and the other reps that have talked. There is another side. Just because we make these chambers available to Will Steger and the crowd that wants to rely on Al Gore's climate porn doesn't mean that that's the way it is. There is another side to the story, one that we tried to present a couple of months ago, but apparently it's frowned upon by the folks that are in control so it doesn't get the same play in this room. Folks, there is another side." [ThinkProgress, 10/13/10]

MISSISSIPPI

Rep. Gregg Harper (R-MS-03): "I don't believe that the science is at all settled on man-made global warming." [Mississippi State University Event, 11/2/12]

MISSOURI

Sen. Roy Blunt (R-MO): "There isn't any real science to say we are altering the climate path of the earth." [Human Events, 4/29/09]

MONTANA

Rep. Ryan Zinke (R-MT-At Large): "It's not a hoax, but it's not proven science either. But you don't dismantle America's power and energy on a maybe. We need to be energy independent first. We need to do it better, which we can, but it is not a settled science." [ThinkProgress, 10/5/14]

Sen. Steve Daines (R-MT-At Large): In a radio interview with Montana Public Radio, Daines admits the climate is changing but questions the impacts by man, that there is "significant debate here," the "jury is still out," and brings up the debate of sun/solar cycles versus greenhouse gases. [Montana Public Radio, 12/2/12]

NEBRASKA

Sen. Deb Fischer (R-NE): "Asked about man-made climate change, Fischer immediately said, "I certainly don't support cap-and-trade.' She said she believes in weather change, but she said she does not believe man has a huge impact on the climate." [The Independent, 8/25/12]

NEVADA

Rep. Mark Amodei (R-NV-02): "The issue of climate change is very controversial and many scientists disagree as to its causes and how to handle it. I recognize that some scientists believe that global warming is caused by failed environmental practices; however, others argue that these temperature increases would incur regardless due to the warming of the center of the earth. I do not believe it is appropriate for the federal government to advocate one position over the other. Since, we do not know much about long-term climate change, I do agree we must have an unbiased research effort funded by both the government and the private sector to answer the essential questions about climate change." [Daily Kos, 8/16/13]

Why Are
Conservatives
Always Wrong?

SCIENCE
AND THE
ENVIRONMENT

NEW HAMPSHIRE

Rep. Frank Guinta (R-NH-01): "I think the science is not complete on this issue. I see different studies that say different things." [Associated Press, 10/7/14]

Sen. Kelly Ayotte (R-NH): Asked if she believed in climate change, she said, "there is scientific evidence that demonstrates there is some impact from human activities. However I don't think the evidence is conclusive." [Sea Coast Online, 9/30/10]

NEW JERSEY

Rep. Scott Garrett (R-NJ-05): "The real question that still exists in a lot of people's minds, experts and non-experts alike, on the area of global warming and what role the government should have in this realm. . . I've heard a number of experts on both sides of the equation on this issue and to me the evidence, the question is still out there." [North Jersey Q&A, 9/30/10]

NEW MEXICO

Rep. Steve Pearce (R-NM-02): "I googled this issue a couple of days ago, see that there are 31,000 scientists who say that human action is not causing the global warming at all. And in fact the last 17 years there has not been global warming, the temperature has been very stable for the last 17 years." [*Mother Jones*, 10/28/14]

NEW YORK

Rep. Lee Zeldin (R-NY-03): "I think it would be very productive if we could just get to exactly what is really and what is not real, because I think both sides of the climate change debate are filled with people who are stretching truths. I'm not sold yet on the whole argument that we have as serious a problem with climate change as other people." [*Newsday*, 10/28/14]

NORTH CAROLINA

Rep. Virginia Foxx (R-NC-05): "North Carolina Republican Virginia Foxx referenced books by climate-change skeptics and lamented that some environmentalists "think that we, human beings, have more impact on the climate and the world than God does." [Huffington Post, 4/7/11]

Rep. Mark Walker (R-NC-06): "We can be green without being extreme. Much of the 'so-called' science of climate change is contested though it's made a few politicians quite wealthy. I believe that God provided the earth to us and we have a responsibility to conserve and respect the environment." [Walker for North Carolina, last accessed 12/8/14]

NORTH DAKOTA

Sen. John Hoeven (R-ND): "Well, the science shows that there's warming. There's different opinions of exactly what's causing it." [Senate Environment and Public Works Committee Hearing]

OHIO

Rep. Bill Johnson (R-OH-06): Johnson asserted in 2011, "I am not an alarmist that believes that greenhouse gas emissions coming from the coal industry are causing major problems." [ThinkProgress, 6/6/13]

OKLAHOMA

Sen. James Lankford (R-OK): "This whole global warming myth will be exposed as what it really is—a way of control more than anything else. And that generation will be ticked." [*Edmond Sun*, 2/16/10]

PENNSYLVANIA

Rep. Lou Barletta (R-PA-11): "You know there's arguments on both sides. I'm not convinced that there's scientific evidence that proves that. I believe there's some that can also argue the opposite." [*Citizens Voice*, 10/17/10]

Rep. Scott Perry (R-PA-04): "I do believe global warming is occurring. . . However, I do take exception, whether it's man-made or not. I learned in public school, the scientific theory. . . You have a theory and it has to be proven. And I'm concerned anytime that a nation, or the world, makes up policy based on a theory that. . . has gained consensus but' does not have proof, he said." [YDR Politics, 9/20/12]

SOUTH CAROLINA

Rep. Trey Gowdy (R-SC-04): "Global warming has not been proven to the satisfaction of the constituents I seek to serve." [Go Upstate, 5/23/10]

Rep. Mick Mulvaney (R-SC-05): "Energy independence, green technology, and innovation is something we should pursue as a nation. However, we shouldn't seek to accomplish that by taxing people based on questionable science. Neither should we ignore domestic energy resources—coal, natural gas, oil—because of baseless claims regarding global warming." [Mulvaney Website]

TENNESSEE

Rep. Marsha Blackburn (R-TN-07): "[T]here is not consensus [on climate change] and you can look at the latest IPCC Report and look at Doctor Lindzen from MIT. His rejection of that or Judith Curry. . . from Georgia Tech. There is not consensus there." [The Wire, 2/17/14]

Why Are
Conservatives
Always Wrong?

SCIENCE
AND THE
ENVIRONMENT

TEXAS

Rep. Joe Barton (R-TX-06): "I don't deny that the climate is changing. I think you can have an honest difference of opinion on what's causing that change without automatically being either all-in that it's all because of mankind or it's all just natural. I think there's a divergence of evidence. . . I would point out if you're a believer in the Bible, one would have to say the Great Flood is an example of climate change. And that certainly wasn't because mankind overdeveloped hydrocarbon energy." [Raw Story, 4/10/13]

Rep. John Carter (R-TX-31): "Global warming is simply a chicken-little scheme to use mass media and government propaganda to convince the world that destruction of individual liberties and national sovereignty is necessary to save mankind, and that the unwashed masses would destroy themselves without the enlightened global dictatorship of these frauds." [Carter Website]

Rep. Bill Flores (R-TX-17): "It is time we stopped putting petty politics based on dubious "agenda-driven, scientific' research ahead of creating more American energy." [Flores Campaign Website, 12/18/11]

Rep. Mac Thornberry (R-TX-13): "Any decisions we make should be based on sound science rather than political, social or personal profit agendas. No computer model yet has correctly predicted the Earth's actual temperatures. We simply do not understand enough about the causes and effects related to our weather." [*USA Today*, 8/10/11]

UTAH

Rep. Chris Stewart (R-UT-02): "The science regarding climate change is anything but settled." [*St. Louis Tribune*, 4/13/13]

VIRGINIA

Rep. J. Randy Forbes (R-VA-04): "Elected officials need to depend on experts in the field to make determinations on the degree to which our planet is warming, and there is evidence among scientists and researchers pointing in both directions." [*Times Dispatch*, 7/4/10]

WASHINGTON

Rep. Cathy McMorris Rodgers (R-WA-05): "We believe Al Gore deserves an 'F' in science and an 'A' in creative writing." [*Whitman Pioneer*, 4/9/09]

WEST VIRGINIA

Rep. David McKinley (R-WV-01): "Many scientists have disavowed past climate change research," McKinley said, and he's waiting for valid science to convince him there's a problem and whether man is to blame. . . "I don't want to listen to Al Gore tell me from a political standpoint that global warming is caused by man because I don't think he can support it."' [Associated Press, 10/20/10]

WISCONSIN

Rep. Paul Ryan (R-WI-01): When asked about humans' role in climate change during a 2014 debate Ryan responded, "I don't know the answer to that question. I don't think science does either." [ThinkProgress, 10/14/14]

WYOMING

Mike Enzi (R-WY): "I barely made it back here because of a May snowstorm in Wyoming. They got 18 inches in Cheyenne. It's a little hard to convince Wyoming people there's global warming. We have 186 percent of normal snow pack. That's global warming?" [Wyoming Public Radio, 5/16/14]

Why Are
Conservatives
Always Wrong?

SCIENCE
AND THE
ENVIRONMENT

what have conservatives said about ...

Natural
Disasters

JOHN HAGEE 2005

RUSH LIMBAUGH 2005

BARBARA BUSH 2005

GEORGE W. BUSH 2005

A firefighter holds an elderly woman rescued from the flood-waters caused by Hurricane Katrina. The elderly made up a good percentage of those stranded by the storm. New Orleans, LA

All hurricanes are acts of
God because God controls
the heavens. I believe that
New Orleans had a level of
sin that was offensive to God
and they were recipients of
the judgment of God for that.

REV. JOHN HAGEE

*Founder and senior pastor of Cornerstone Church
in San Antonio, Texas, on Hurricane Katrina, 2005*

*Members of the FEMA Urban Search and Rescue
task forces help stranded Hurricane Katrina survivors
reach dry land. New Orleans, LA, August 31, 2005*

I mean, why didn't these morons leave New Orleans before the hurricane? I'll tell you why: because they wanted to rape and loot! That's just the way some people are! And if they're black—if the rapists and looters are black—it's not George Bush's fault! We've had these problems ever since the Emancipation Proclamation.

RUSH LIMBAUGH

Radio talk show host, writer, and conservative political commentator, 2005

A Red Cross volunteer comforts a survivor from Hurricane
Katrina in the Houston Astrodome, September 2, 2005

So many of the people in the arena here, you know, were underprivileged anyway, so this is working very well for them.

BARBARA BUSH

*Touring the Hurricane Katrina refugee
camp at the Houston Astrodome, 2005*

Brownie, you're doing a heckuva job!

GEORGE W. BUSH

*President of the United States, to FEMA
director, Michael Brown, in the aftermath
of Hurricane Katrina, 2005*

Epilogue

The Beatles are not merely awful. They are so unbelievably horrible, so appallingly unmusical, so dogmatically insensitive to the magic of the art, that they qualify as crowned heads of antimusic.

WILLIAM F. BUCKLEY JR.
Founder of the National Review *and conservative commentator, 1964*

Special Thanks

So much of the sense and meaning of this book is conveyed graphically and aesthetically through design. In that, I had amazing partners. I want to thank Kristen Weber for the interior book design and Ann Weinstock for the cover design. This book looks as gorgeous as it does because of them. I'd also like to extend my special thanks to Mary Bisbee-Beek for her direction and counsel. Every book needs a guide, including finding the team of Kristen and Ann, and she did it with wit and wisdom. I'm grateful to Jess Kibler for her photo research. Her accuracy and thoroughness was appreciated and admired.

It was so much fun and so much pleasure to work with you all.

Credits

SLAVERY

Page 2   James H. Hammond. Library of Congress, Prints and Photographs Division, LC-DIG-ppmsca-26689.

Page 4   John C. Calhoun. Photograph by Matthew B. Brady. Library of Congress Prints and Photographs Division, Brady-Handy Photograph Collection, LC-USZ62-10556.

Page 6   Union soldiers protecting the young woman whom they helped escape slavery. Photograph by James Presley Ball, September 1862. Library of Congress Prints and Photographs Division, Gladstone Collection of African American Photographs, LC-DIG-ppmsca-10940.

Page 8   Sojourner Truth. Library of Congress Prints and Photographs Division, Gladstone Collection of African American Photographs, LC-DIG-ppmsca-08978.

Page 10   Jefferson Davis. Library of Congress, Prints and Photographs Division, Brady-Handy Collection, LC-DIG-cwpbh-00879.

Page 12   Samuel F.B. Morse. Library of Congress, Prints and Photographs Division, LC-USZ62-2188.

Page 14   Alexander Stephens. Library of Congress Prints and Photographs Division, Brady-Handy Photograph Collection, LC-BH832-304.

Page 16   Woodrow Wilson. Library of Congress, Prints and Photographs Division, LC-USZ62-56194.

Page 18   Scars of a whipped Mississippi slave, photographed April 2, 1863, Baton Rouge, Louisiana. National Archives and Records Administration, 533232.

NATIVE AMERICANS

Page 22   George Washington. Painting by Rembrandt Peale, The Athenaeum.

Page 24   Thomas Jefferson. Painting by Rembrandt Peale, The White House Historical Association (White House Collection).

Why Are
Conservatives
Always Wrong?

Page 26   John Marshall. Print by J.H.E. Whitney after St. Mamin, ca. January 29, 1889. Library of Congress Prints and Photographs Division , LC-USZ62-8499.

Page 28   Andrew Jackson. Library of Congress Prints and Photographs Division, LC-USZ62-13007.

Page 30   Theodore Roosevelt in uniform. Library of Congress Prints and Photographs Division, LC-DIG-ppmsca-36046.

Page 32   Theodore Roosevelt. Library of Congress Prints and Photographs Division, LC-DIG-cwpbh-03437.

IMPERIALISM AND THE AMERICAN EMPIRE

Page 36   Filipino casualties on the first day of the Philippine-American War, February 5, 1899. National Archives and Records Administration, Greely Collection, 524389.

Page 38   U.S. soldiers in Manilla, during the Philippine-American war, ca. 1899. Library of Congress, Prints and Photographs Division, LC-USZ61-957.

Page 40   Albert Beveridge. Library of Congress, Prints and Photographs Division, George Grantham Bain Collection, LC-DIG-ggbain-05037.

Page 42   Oregon Volunteer Infantry on firing line outside of Pasig, Philippine Islands, March 14, 1899. National Archives and Records Administration, Office of the Chief Signal Officer, 530692.

WOMEN'S SUFFRAGE

Page 46   Woodrow Wilson, Mr. and Mrs. Woodrow Wilson seated outdoors with their three daughters standing behind them: (left to right) Margaret, Eleanor, and Jessie, in Cornish, New Hampshire, 1912. Photograph by Pach Brothers. Library of Congress Prints and Photographs Division, LC-USZ62-7633.

Page 48   Charles Carter. Library of Congress, Prints and Photographs Division, Harris & Ewing Collection, LC-DIG-hec-21020.

Page 50   Women's suffrage headquarters, Cleveland, Ohio. Library of Congress, Prints and Photographs Division, LC-USZ62-30776.

Page 52   Frank Clark. Library of Congress, Prints and Photographs Division, George Grantham Bain Collection, LC-USZ62-111670.

Page 54   Edwin Webb. Library of Congress, Prints and Photographs Division, George Grantham Bain Collection, LC-DIG-ggbain-12921.

Page 56   Stanley Bowdle. Library of Congress, Prints and Photographs Division, Harris & Ewing Collection, LC-DIG-hec-17524.

Page 58 *The Age of Brass*. Currier & Ives etching, 1869. Library of Congress, Prints and Photographs Division, LC-DIG-pga-05762.

JIM CROW AND SEGREGATION

Page 62 Roger B. Taney. Library of Congress Prints and Photographs Division, Brady-Handy Photograph Collection, LC-DIG-cwpbh-00789.

Page 64 Benjamin Tillman. Photograph by G. V. Buck. Library of Congress, Prints and Photographs Division, LC-USZ62-104434.

Page 66 President Roosevelt and Booker Washington reviewing the sixty-one "industry" floats, Tuskegee, AL, January 12, 1906. Library of Congress Prints and Photographs Division, LC-DIG-stereo-1s02155.

Page 68 James Kimble Vardaman. Library of Congress Prints and Photographs Division, National Photo Company Collection, LC-DIG-npcc-20187.

Page 70 Group of hooded Ku Klux Klan members posed in shape of a cross in front of tent, ca. January 2, 1924. Library of Congress Prints and Photographs Division, LC-USZ62-77228.

Page 72 Woodrow Wilson. Library of Congress, Prints and Photographs Division, Harris & Ewing Collection, LC-USZC2-6247.

Page 74 Theodore G. Bilbo. Library of Congress Prints and Photographs Division, Harris & Ewing Collection, LC-DIG-hec-19313.

Page 76 Filibuster against anti-lynching bill. Washington, D.C., Janurary 27, 1938. Members of the bloc of Southern Senators who have been filibusting against the anti-lynching bill for the last twenty days and are still going strong, left to right: Senator Tom Connaly, of Texas, Sen. Walter F. George, of Ga.; Sen. Richard Russell of Ga.; and Sen. Claude Pepper of Florida. Library of Congress Prints and Photographs Division, Harris & Ewing Collection, LC-DIG-hec-23959.

Page 78 Burnet R. Maybank. Library of Congress Prints and Photographs Division, Harris & Ewing Collection, LC-DIG-hec-27534.

Page 80 Eugene Talmadge. Surprise visit from Georgia. Gov. Eugene Talmadge, of Georgia, consistent New Deal critic as he paid a surprise visit to Pres. Roosevelt at the White House Wednesday. Gov. Talmadge, in a cream colored suit, and red suspenders, indicated surprise when confonted by newsmen and photographers. "How did you know I was coming here" he asked. He was accompanied by Clark Howell, Atlanta, Ga., publisher. The two men are seen here leaving the White House, Gov. Talmadge at right, July 17, 1935. Library of Congress, Prints and Photographs Division, Harris & Ewing Collection, LC-DIG-hec-39250.

Page 82   Allen Joseph Ellender. Photograph by Underwood and Underwood, Library of Congress, Prints and Photographs Division, LC-USZ62-73776.

Page 84   Strom Thrumond. Library of Congress, Prints and Photographs Division, U.S. News & World Report Magazine Photograph Collection, LC-DIG-ppmsca-19604.

Page 86   School integration conflicts, Clinton, TN, December 4, 1956. Library of Congress Prints and Photographs Division, U.S. News & World Report Magazine Photograph Collection, LC-DIG-ppmsca-03089.

Page 88   George C. Wallace. Photograph showing Gov. Wallace standing defiantly at a door while being confronted by Deputy U.S. Attorney General Nicholas Katzenbach. Library of Congress, Prints and Photographs Division, U.S. News & World Report Magazine Photograph Collection, LC-DIG-ppmsca-04294.

IMMIGRATION

Page 92   Four Chinese men with percussion instruments, March 15, 1904. Library of Congress Prints and Photographs Division , LC-USZ62-53833.

Page 94   Theodore Roosevelt speaking at the back of a railroad car, May 25, 1907. Underwood & Underwood. Library of Congress Prints and Photographs Division, LC-DIG-ppmsca-36689.

Page 96   Italian family living in New York City, NY. Photographed by Lewis Wickes Hine, December 1911. Library of Congress, Prints & Photographs Division, National Child Labor Committee Collection, Lewis Hine, LC-DIG-nclc-04116.

Page 98   Woodrow Wilson. Photograph by Pach Brothers. Library of Congress, Prints and Photographs Division, LC-USZ62-132907.

Page 100   Calvin Coolidge. Photograph by Notman Photo Co., Library of Congress, Prints and Photographs Division, LC-DIG-ppmsc-03670.

Page 102   Ellis Island, immigrant children. Photograph by Brown Brothers, ca. 1908. National Archives and Records Administration, Records of the Public Health Service. Created for the Department of the Treasury, Public Health Service, 6341034.

Page 104   Chinese-American girl playing hopscotch with American friends outside her home in Flatbush, New York, New York. Photographed by Marjory Collins, August 1942. Library of Congress, Prints & Photographs Division, Farm Security Administration – Office of War Information Photograph Collection, LC-DIG-fsa-8d21950.

Page 108   Donald Trump. Gage Skidmore via Creative Commons Attribution-Share Alike 3.0 Unported License: https://creativecommons.org/licenses/by-sa/3.0/legalcode.

CIVIL RIGHTS

Page 112   William Rehnquist. Library of Congress, Prints and Photographs Division, LC-USZ62-60141.

Page 114   Little Rock, August 20, 1959: Rally at state capitol Photograph showing a group of people, several holding signs and American flags, protesting the admission of the "Little Rock Nine" to Central High School. Library of Congress Prints and Photographs Division, U.S. News & World Report Magazine Photograph Collection, LC-DIG-ppmsca-19754.

Page 116   Martin Luther King, Jr. marching with leaders in March on Washington, 1963. Library of Congress Prints and Photographs Division, U.S. News & World Report Magazine Photograph Collection, LC-DIG-ppmsca-37253.

Page 118   Martin Luther King, Jr., at freedom rally, Washington Temple Church. World Telegram & Sun photo by O. Fernandez. Staff photographer reproduction rights transferred to Library of Congress through Instrument of Gift. Library of Congress, Prints & Photographs Division, NYWT&S Collection, LC-USZ62-111157.

Page 120   "No More Birminghams." Congress of Racial Equality conducts march in memory of Negro youngsters killed in Birmingham bombings, All Souls Church, 16th Street, Washington, D.C., September 22, 1963. Photograph by Thomas J. O'Halloran. Library of Congress Prints and Photographs Division, U.S. News & World Report Magazine Photograph Collection, LC-DIG-ppmsca-04298.

Page 122   Ronald Reagan. Photograph by Michael Evans, 1976. National Archives and Records Administration, 198600.

Page 124   Lee Atwater "jams" with President George H.W. Bush at Inaugural festivity. Official White House Photograph, January 21, 1989, P0142-22.

Page 126   President Ronald Reagan motioning to Ed Meese during a White House Press Briefing on Iran-Contra, November 25, 1986. National Archives and Records Administration, 198579.

Page 132   William Bennett. Gage Skidmore via Creative Commons Attribution-Share Alike 3.0 Unported License: https://creativecommons.org/licenses/by-sa/3.0/legalcode.

Page 134   Alberto Gonzales. Courtesy of the U.S. Department of Justice.

FREEDOM TO MARRY

Page 138   Roger B. Taney. Library of Congress Prints and Photographs Division, Brady-Handy Photograph Collection, LC-DIG-cwpbh-00789.

Page 140   James R. Doolittle. Library of Congress, Prints and Photographs Division, Brady-Handy Collection, LC-DIG-cwpbh-00204.

Page 144   Frederic Douglass Frederick with his wife, Helen Pitts Douglass (seated, right), and her sister Eva Pitts (standing, center). Courtesy of the National Park Service.

Page 150   "We Love Our Daughter and Her Wife." Recently married couple with supportive mother on the steps of City Hall, San Francisco, CA. June 17, 2008. Photograph by Marc Love. Licensed via Creative Commons Attribution-ShareAlike 2.0 Generic license: https://creativecommons.org/licenses/by-sa/2.0/legalcode.

Page 152   Marriage Equality Rally at the U.S. Supreme Court on First Street between Maryland Avenue and East Capitol Street, NE, Washington, D.C. on Tuesday morning, March 26. 2013. Photograph by Elvert Barnes Protest Photography. Licensed via Creative Commons ShareAlike 2.0 Generic. license: https://creativecommons.org/licenses/by-sa/2.0/legalcode.

Page 154   Recently married couples leaving the City Hall in Seattle, WA, are greeted by well-wishers on the first day of same-sex marriage in Washington state after enactment of Washington Referendum 74. December 9, 2012. Photograph by Dennis Bratland. Licensed via Creative Commons Attribution-Share Alike 3.0 Unported license https://creativecommons.org/licenses/by-sa/3.0/deed.en.

Page 156   SCOTUS APRIL 2015 LGBTQ 54663 Arguments at the United States Supreme Court for Same-Sex Marriage on April 28, 2015. Photograph by Ted Eytan. Creative Commons Attribution-Share Alike 2.0 Generic license: https://creativecommons.org/licenses/by-sa/2.0/legalcode.

Page 158   Marriage Equality Rally at the U.S. Supreme Court on First Street between Maryland Avenue and East Capitol Street, NE, Washington, D.C. on Tuesday morning, March 26. 2013. Photograph by Elvert Barnes Protest Photography. Licensed via Creative Commons ShareAlike 2.0 Generic. license: https://creativecommons.org/licenses/by-sa/2.0/legalcode.

SEXUAL PRIVACY

Page 162   "Gay Rights Are Human Rights." Captial Pride Parade, June 11, 2011. Photograph by ep_jhu. Licensed via Creative Commons Attribution-ShareAlike 2.0 Generic license: https://creativecommons.org/licenses/by-sa/2.0/legalcode.

Page 166   Patrick Buchanan. July 12, 1969. Richard Nixon Presidential Library and Museum. National Archives and Records Administration, 194638.

WOMEN'S BODIES AND RIGHTS

Page 178   Dick Armey. Gage Skidmore via Creative Commons Attribution-Share Alike 2.0 Generic License: https://creativecommons.org/licenses/by-sa/2.0/legalcode.

Page 180   Todd Akin. KOMUnews via Creative Commons Attribution 2.0 Generic License: https://creativecommons.org/licenses/by/2.0/legalcode.

Page 182   Rick Santorum. Gage Skidmore via Creative Commons Attribution–Share Alike 3.0 Unported License: https://creativecommons.org/licenses/by-sa/3.0/legalcode.

Page 184   Richard Mourdock. Official portrait courtesy of the State of Indiana.

RICHARD NIXON

Page 188   Richard Nixon. Department of Defense, National Archives and Records Administration, 530679.

Page 190   President Richard Nixon, with edited transcripts of Nixon White House Tape conversations during broadcast of his address to the Nation announcing his resignation, April 29, 1974. National Archives & Records Administration, WHPO C1269-20.

RELIGION AND GOVERNMENT

Page 196   Sunday morning. Dayton, TN. This was the town in which the famous Scopes trial (*Tennessee v. John Thomas Scopes*, commonly referred to as the Scopes Monkey Trial) was held in 1925. Photograph by Dorthea Lange, July 1936. Library of Congress, Prints & Photographs Division, Farm Security Administration - Office of War Information Photograph Collection, LC-USF34- 009566-C.

WAR

Page 202   Ronald Reagan. Official portrait, April 8, 1981. Courtesy of the Ronald Reagan Presidential Library & Museum.

Page 204   173 Airborne Brigade in a firefight on Hill 823 during the Vietnam War. Photograph by U.S. Army.

Page 206   George W. Bush. Official portrait courtesy of the United States Department of Defense, ID 030114-O-0000D-001_screen.

Page 210   General Lee lies on its side after surviving a buried IED blast on April 15, 2007. The Stryker was recovered and protected its soldiers on more missions until another bomb finally put it out of action. Photograph courtesy of U.S. Army. Licensed under the Creative Commons Attribution 2.0 Generic license, https://creativecommons.org/licenses/by/2.0/deed.en.

Page 212   Donald Rumsfeld. Photograph by Tech. Sgt. Andy Dunaway, October 8, 2003. Courtesy of the U.S. Department of Defense, U.S. Navy, ID 031008-F-2828D-057.

Page 214   Dick Cheney. Official portrait courtesy of the United States Department of Defense, U.S. Airforce.

Page 216   Dick Cheney. Vice President delivers the commencement at the U.S. Naval Academy's 2006 Graduation and Commissioning Ceremony. U.S. Navy photo by Chief Photographer's Mate Johnny Bivera, Annapolis, MD, May 26, 2006. Courtesy of the United States Navy with the ID 060526-N-2383B-270.

Page 218   Ground Zero, aerial view. Photograph by Chief Photographer's Mate Eric J. Tilford, September 17, 2001. U.S. Department of Defense, U.S. Navy, ID 010917-N-7479T-515.

ECONOMIC REGULATION

Page 222   George F. Edmunds. Library of Congress, Prints and Photographs Division, Brady-Handy Collection, LC-DIG-cwpbh-05024.

Page 224   Addie Card. 12 year old spinner in North Pownal Cotton Mill. VT. Photograph by Lewis Wickes Hine, February 1910. Library of Congress, Prints & Photographs Division, National Child Labor Committee Collection, LC-DIG-nclc-01830.

Page 226   Tenement homework. Of a family of 7 children, all but 2 work stringing tags. The oldest child is 12. A little fellow who looked about 6 was quite an expert. The children received 20 cents for stringing a thousand tage [i.e., tags] - they tie a knot in a piece of string, and run the string thru [sic] the tag. They moisten the ends of their fingers in their mouths to tie the knots. They can string about a thousand tags in half an hour. .Newark, NJ. Photograph by Lewis Wickes Hine, 1923. Library of Congress, Prints & Photographs Division, National Child Labor Committee Collection, LC-DIG-nclc-04321.

Page 228   Ewin L. Davis. Library of Congress, Prints and Photographs Division, Harris & Ewing Collection, LC-DIG-hec-19366.

Page 230   Oklahoma migratory workers washing in a hot spring in the desert. Imperial Valley, California. Photograph by Dorthea Lange, March 1937. Library of Congress, Prints & Photographs Division, Farm Security Administration - Office of War Information Photograph Collection, LC-DIG-fsa-8b31863.

Page 232   Alf Landon. Repub. nominee for presidency in 1936, facing a battery of cameras when he arrived at White House for luncheon conference with Pres. Roosevelt ca. 1940. Library of Congress Prints and Photographs Division, Harris & Ewing Collection, LC-DIG-hec-28693.

Page 234   Edward Cox. Library of Congress, Prints and Photographs Division, Harris & Ewing Collection, LC-DIG-hec-26376.

Page 236   Billboard on U.S. Highway 99 in California. National advertising campaign sponsored by the National Association of Manufacturers. Photograph by Dorothea Lange, March 1937. Library of Congress Prints and Photographs Division, U.S. Farm

Security Administration/Office of War Information Black & White Photographs, LC-USF34-016213-C.

Page 238   Ronald and Nancy Reagan at the Victory celebration for California Governor at the Biltmore Hotel in Los Angeles, California. November 8, 1966. Courtesy Ronald Reagan Presidential Library & Museum.

Page 240   Alan Greenspan testifying before the House Senate Economic Committee, Washington, D.C., January 6, 1975. Library of Congress, Prints and Photographs Division, U.S. News & World Report Magazine Photograph Collection, LC-DIG-ds-03243.

Page 242   Ronald Reagan in the White House Oval Office during his last term, Washington, D.C., 1986. Photographs in the Carol M. Highsmith Archive, Library of Congress, Prints and Photographs Division, LC-DIG-highsm-14732.

Page 246   Alan Greenspan. Portrait courtesy of the Bureau of Engraving and Printing.

SCIENCE AND THE ENVIRONMENT

Page 250   Harshaw Chemical Company discharges industrial waste water into the Cuyahoga River. Photograph by Frank J. (Frank John) Aleksandrowicz, May, 1973. National Archives and Records Administration, Records of the Environmental Protection Agency, NWDNS-412-DA-7708.

Page 252   Ronald and Nancy Reagan waving from the limousine during the Inaugural Parade in Washington, D.C. on Inauguration Day, January 1,1981. White House Photographic Office. National Archives and Records Administration, 198507.

Page 254   Southbound Interstate 95 approaching the exit for Girard Avenue/Lehigh Avenue (exit 23) in Philadelphia, Pennsylvania, July 23, 2008. Photograph by Dough4872. The photographer has released this work into the public domain.

Page 256   Lee Iacocca. Library of Congress, Prints and Photographs Division, US News & World Report Magazine Photograph Collection, LC-DIG-ds-07053.

Page 262   Dick Cheney. Official portrait courtesy of the United States Department of Defense, U.S. Airforce.

Page 264   James Inhofe. Official senate portrait courtesy of the United States government, 2007.

Page 266   Michelle Bachmann. Official congressional portrait courtesy of the United States government, 2011.

Page 268   Jeff Sessions. Official senate portrait courtesy of the United States government.

Page 270   The 2011 Texas drought dried up much of Central Texas water ways. This boat was left to sit in the middle of what is normally a branch of Lake Travis, part of the Colorado River. July 17, 2011. Phototgraph by Erik A. Ellison. Licensed under the Creative Commons Attribution-Share Alike 3.0 Unported license.

NATURAL DISASTERS

Page 282   A firefighter holds an elderly woman rescued from the floodwaters caused by Hurricane Katrina. The elderly made up a good percentage of those stranded by the storm. The City of New Orleans is being evacuated following hurricane Katrina. New Orleans, LA, August 31, 2005. Photograph by Win Henderson / FEMA.

Page 284   Members of the FEMA Urban Search and Rescue task forces continue to help residents impacted by Hurricane Katrina. These residents were transported to the area from various neighborhoods and need to cross over the tracks to get on a second boat which will bring them to dry land. New Orleans, LA, August 31, 2005. Photograph by Jocelyn Augustino / FEMA.

Page 286   A Red Cross volunteer comforts a survivor from Hurricane Katrina in the Houston Astrodome. Approximately 18,000 people are temporarily housed in the Red Cross shelter at the Astrodome and Reliant center. The City of New Orleans is being evacuated following Hurricane Katrina and rising flood waters. Houston, TX, September 2, 2005. Photo by Andrea Booher / FEMA.

Page 288   George. W. Bush. Official portrait courtesy of the United States Department of Defense, ID 030114-O-0000D-001_screen.